MODERN WAR
AND THE
AMERICAN CHURCHES

MODERN WAR AND THE AMERICAN CHURCHES

A Factual Study of
the Christian Conscience on Trial
From 1939 to the Cold War Crisis of Today

by

Ralph Luther Moellering, M.A., S.T.M.

THE AMERICAN PRESS   NEW YORK, N. Y.

Library of Congress Catalog Card Number: 56–9006

FIRST EDITION

THE AMERICAN PRESS   489 Fifth Avenue   New York 17, N.Y.

MANUFACTURED IN THE UNITED STATES OF AMERICA

To my parents

whose sacrifice and inspiration made my education possible, this book is gratefully and affectionately dedicated.

Acknowledgments are due to Dr. A. M. Rehwinkel, Professor of Christian Ethics at Concordia Seminary, St. Louis, for encouragement in pursuing this study; to my brother, the Reverend H. Armin Moellering, of Palisades Park, New Jersey, for offering me the use of his files, and for providing an English translation of the quotations from the Latin of John Gerhard; to numerous publishers cited in the Notes for the permission which they have kindly tendered to quote from their publications; and to my wife for patiently typing the manuscript and assisting in the necessary research.

Contents

Contents

MODERN WAR
AND THE
AMERICAN CHURCHES

Preface

The author felt impelled to do the research for this book because of his own misgivings regarding the wisdom and justice of American involvement in the Second World War. The ready compliance of most churches with whatever was demanded by government decree or popular sentiment appeared to him to represent a surrender of Christian witness. The apparent acceptance by much of the clergy of everything that happened, no matter how vile and inhumane, as a sort of inevitable concomitant of war, was a source of deep concern to him. The cruel excesses and the mass slaughter of whole populations did not seem to elicit the compassion one would expect from those who claimed Christ as their Head. Sometimes hatred and vengeance were actually promoted in ecclesiastical quarters. Where there was not enthusiastic endorsement of the military, there was usually submissive conformity.

Underlying the attitudes which prevailed were traditions of unquestioning obedience to government, an extreme view of the separation of church and state, and avowed Christian support for what is called a "just war." The writer is convinced that these concepts need to be judiciously scrutinized and carefully re-evaluated. A number of thorough studies should be made to determine wherein we failed to fulfill our obligations as church leaders and laymen in both World War II and the Korean War, so that we can better discharge our Christian responsibilities in the present world situation.

It should be stated here, however, that the author has made every effort to present an objective and unbiased account of how the major church bodies *did* react to the problem of Christian participation in war. In most instances the treatment of a denomination has been read and checked by clergymen of the communion under consideration; and in every instance where this has been done, the individuals consulted have agreed that the presentation is accurate and fair. If more space has been allotted to the Lutheran Church than her total membership would seem to warrant, it is because this is the communion with which the author is most familiar by personal affiliation, and which has, at least until recently, preserved the most uncritical attitude in relation to the question of Christian support of modern war. The studies produced by the World Council of Churches, and the pronouncements of such nondenominational journals as *Christianity and Crisis* and *The Christian Century* do not fall within the compass of this book. Limiting the scope of investigation has also ruled out a consideration of Baptist opinion, as well as of the opinion of the many smaller and diverse Pentecostal and Holiness bodies.

Since the Lutheran Church accepts the Holy Scriptures as the only rightful norm and source for faith and life, and since most other Christians also claim to derive their convictions at least to some extent from this Source, I have introduced my study with a brief examination of the material pertinent to the problem of war and peace in the two Testaments. Militarists, as well as some church groups, are quick to "exploit" the Old Testament as an *apologia* for the stand they take. Christian pacifists, vocal and demonstrative throughout the Second World War, made a continuous appeal to the New Testament and the teachings of Jesus.

Naturally, the conclusions drawn by the writer are subjective to the extent that they are based on his own findings, and no one person can pretend to be cognizant of all the data that would be relevant to a study so comprehensive in scope. Nor would he deny that his ultimate aim in offering this volume is didactic and hortative. It is the author's intention to point out some of the shortcomings and past mistakes of the established churches, but also to indicate what he believes to be certain correctives and safeguards for the future.

1

Militarism in the Old Testament?

Those Christians who are committed to the orthodox conception of Biblical inspiration have always defended the authenticity and canonicity of the Old Testament. The New Testament writers, they point out, always assume that the sacred books of the Hebrews are reliable and God-given. Both Peter and Paul are emphatic in their assurance that Scripture was inspired by the Holy Spirit in a unique manner that would imply the full accuracy of the records. The Gospel narratives present Jesus as giving the stamp of approval to the writings of Moses and the Prophets.

Many modern theologians, including a number of ardent pacifists, have sidestepped the problem of militarism in the Old Testament by subscribing in greater or lesser degree to the contentions of critics who call into question the historicity of the stories and look upon the Judaic ethic as exhibiting a gradual development from a lower to a higher plane. They do not feel obliged to defend or explain the wars of Israel, for they can be dismissed as the skirmishes of a semicivilized people or as evidences of an extreme nationalism that led to fanatical outbursts of ferocity.

Lord Raglan, a British scientist, addressing the Society of Friends, insisted that the Old Testament was undesirable for youthful readers:

> Moses, David, Samuel, Joshua, and others were monsters of aggression, cruelty, and atrocities unequalled in any modern conflicts. The fact that such cruelty both in peace and war was characteristic of the times and countries in

which these Bible heroes lived, may explain them to an anthropologist, but does not excuse us in using them as examples of manliness and morality before the young people.[1]

Citations from the Old Testament are usually evaded, by such critics, by relegating them to the pre-Christian era. When Christ came, it is urged, He manifested a new ethic of nonresistance which was alien to the authors of the historical books, such as Judges or Kings, but which was at least partially anticipated in the lofty pronouncements of the Prophets. One leading pacifist has contended: "The God of Jesus differs fundamentally from the Jehovah presented in many sections of the Old Testament where Jehovah is frequently pictured as authorizing pillage and slaughter, and often as Himself an active participant." [2]

There is no denying that war in the Old Testament is a gruesome business that causes manifold problems for Christian interpreters. The pages of Hebrew history are red with the blood of God's saints, who, in turn, wreaked havoc among their enemies. None of the gory details are spared. Man's inhumanity to man is redundantly displayed. Some of the revolting horrors are so vividly portrayed that some Bible critics have called for an expurgated edition.

The Book of Joshua, for instance, records the utter annihilation of the heathen inhabitants of Canaan. All the military tactics and strategy are outlined. Sometimes the populations of whole cities were exterminated, it would appear. In a desert battle "they [the Israelites] slew them until not one remained or escaped." Men and women were put to the sword. "Joshua did not withdrew his hand . . . until he had massacred all the inhabitants of Ai" (Josh. 8:26).[3] In the same way, when the Hebrew general captured Makkedah no one was spared. Both the king of that city and his subjects were killed. Then, as the Israelite armies advance and the conquest proceeds, the refrain is repeated: "He put them to the sword, and massacred every person that was in it, sparing no one." A total of thirty-one vanquished kings is listed in this manner.

After the death of Joshua, we are told, the tribes of Judah and Simeon continued the attacks on the Canaanites to safeguard their borders from molesting heathen. Not content with mere victory, they resorted to cruelty. The captured Adoni-bezek, with his thumbs and big toes cut off, bemoaned his fate as the same as that which had been meted out to seventy other kings (Judg. 1:4ff). While Deborah, the prophetess, was governing Israel, it is related that a woman by the name of Jael took a hammer and drove a tent peg through the forehead of Sisera, the Canaanite general, while pretending to be his benefactor.

When the Moabites imposed their suzerainty on Israel, Ehud played a dastardly role. After paying the required tribute to Eglon, King of Moab, he coaxed him into a private audience, "and drawing the dagger from his right hip, he plunged it into his abdomen, so that the hilt also went in after the blade and the fat closed over the blade . . ." [3] (Judg. 3:21ff).

After Gideon's nocturnal invasion had caused consternation in the camp of the Midianites, the Ephraimites joined in the rout and captured the two leading chieftains of the enemy. As trophies of the war they brought their heads to Gideon. Later, when the officials of Succoth refused to give provisions to his exhausted army, Gideon seized them and trampled them into the desert thorns and briers (Judg. 8:5). In civil conflict Jephthah rallied the Gileadites to defeat the Ephraimites. Forty-two thousand were identified and slain at the fords of the Jordan River when they could not pronounce "shibboleth" correctly (Judg. 12:4ff).

In a fit of anger Samson killed and despoiled thirty Philistines to "pay off a bet" (Judg. 14:19). Because his wife was taken away and given to a rival, he took revenge on the Philistines and burned their crops. After killing a thousand Philistines who had attempted to capture him, Samson boasted with a cry of triumph: "With the red ass's jawbone I have dyed them red; with the red ass's jawbone I have felled a thousand men" (Judg. 15:16).

The crime of Gibeah provoked a furious vengeance upon the tribe of Benjamin. The ensuing battle scenes are depicted in full horror. During the first and second days of the fighting the ranks of the Israelites were decimated by thirty thousand deaths. On the third day twenty-five thousand Benjaminites were slaughtered. Before the carnage ended, it is reported that the Israelites turned their attention to the civilian population and "put to the sword both man and beast, and everything that was to be found; all the cities too . . . they set on fire" (Judg. 20:48).

Bloodshed and conflict continued after the establishment of the monarchy. Saul and David were revered because they were capable warriors. And often their campaign strategy was based on the ruthless total destruction of the opposing forces. Following up on advantages gained during the day, Saul recommended to his army: "Let us go down after the Philistines by night and plunder among them until dawn, and let us not leave a man of them" (I Sam. 14:36).

A particularly vicious act seems to have been perpetrated when Samuel had the king of the Amalekites at his mercy. The trembling Agag was hewed in pieces "before the Lord in Gilgal." Even David's slaying of Goliath must appear truculent as well as valiant. The stone sank into the giant's forehead and the youth cut off his head. Hatred against the Philistines had become so intense that David did not hesitate to kill a hundred Philistines in order to acquire Saul's daughter, Michal, as his wife. Little value seems to have been placed on the human character of these heathen; the narratives of these expeditions sound almost like stories of hunters bringing in the pelts of hundreds of fur-bearing animals. During the period of David's banishment and seclusion, he led his band of men in specific attacks against different tribes. He did not spare the women and he confiscated all the wealth he could (cf. I Sam. 27:9ff).

After David's ascendance to the throne, the bitter warfare continued. After subduing the Philistines, he defeated the Moabites "and measured them off with a line, making them lie down on the ground; and he measured two lines to put to death and one line to save alive" (II Sam. 8:2). The Syrians made a futile attempt to forestall the expansion of the Hebrew Empire. When they rushed to the assistance of Hadadezer, King of Zobah, twenty-two thousand were slain.

Centuries later, under King Amaziah in the Southern Kingdom, an especially odious atrocity was committed. Ninety thousand men of Seir were killed in battle, and ten thousand more were captured. The prisoners were promptly hustled to the top of a precipice and hurled down, "so that all of them were dashed to pieces" (II Chron. 25:11*ff*).

This history of Israel reeks with violence and turbulence. When God's People were not engaged in combat with an alien power, they were involved in internecine strife.

Why all this bloodshed in a Book that purports to come from God? This is not a simple problem for the modern reader; it cannot be lightly dismissed. But at least a partial answer is to be found in the Apostolic reminder that "whatever was written in former days was written for our instruction" (Rom. 15:4 RSV). The repetitious recital of wars and cruelties in the Old Testament should be nauseating to the regenerated Christian. Nevertheless, it is a realistic portrayal of what actually happened. Dehumanized men gave vent to their homicidal instincts. Then, as now, war was hell on earth. To gloss it over, to omit even the most shocking episodes, might cause us to underestimate the depths of the depravity to which man can sink. The Biblical writers are concerned with relating enough about the insane antics of war-frenzied men to show the ultimate result of rebellion against God.

Then, too, we need not assume that every brutality recorded and every battle fought met with divine approval, any more than did the immorality and idolatry which is cited time after time in the same Book. Occasionally war was due to the blunders of individual leaders. Often it was caused by the folly and stubborn waywardness of Israel as a whole people. As Paul told the Corinthian congregation: "Now these things happened to them as a warning, but they were written down for our instruction, upon whom the end of the ages has come" (I Cor. 10:11 RSV).

In historical retrospect Moses reminded his people that they had once scorned the injunction of the Lord and recklessly lunged into the highlands of the Amorites, only to be chased back in disgrace (Deut. 1:41-46).

Certainly, another basic key to an understanding of how war could be sanctioned, and even commanded, in the Old Testament lies in the attribute of God's justice. God cannot condone sin. His holy nature obliges Him to use punitive measures in effacing evil. Many calamities since the Fall of man have been manifestations of

God's retributive justice. The Deluge of Noah's day was provoked by the appalling wickedness of men. The confusion of tongues at the Tower of Babel and the subsequent scattering abroad were occasioned by the proud and rebellious spirit of man. In a similar way earthquakes, droughts, and epidemics are mentioned in the Bible as the media through which God's displeasure over human iniquity is revealed. The most recurrent catastrophe through which God castigated human depravity was war. All the bloodshed and heartache incurred by the ravages of war emphasize the gravity of sin and the folly of man's persistent attempt to rule God out of his affairs.

A morally sensitive person would quite naturally inquire, however: "Why did God command the annihilation of the inhabitants of Canaan? How could He endorse the harsh brutality that occurred?" This may indeed seem inexplicable unless we recall that God has the sovereign right to punish evil. Just as the immoral perversions of Sodom and Gomorrah reeked to high heaven and called down upon the populace fire and brimstone, so the abhorrent pagan rites of the Canaanites summoned purgation by sword and merciless attack.[4] Evidently God wanted to wipe out all the traces of degeneracy in the territory where His Chosen People would live. It is expressly stated that "it is because of the wickedness of these nations that the Lord your God is about to drive them out of your way" (Deut. 9:5).

Earlier in the perambulations along the border a thousand troops from each tribe had been mobilized "to execute the Lord's vengeance on Midian" (Num. 31:2-4). There was a frightful carnage in which every male enemy was slain. But warfare was now being commanded again because of the vile conspiracy of the Midianites to have Israelite men seduced by Moabite women (*cf.* Num. 25:16-18).

But what aggravates the difficulties of interpretation for the Christian theologian is the apparently close relationship between the evils of warfare and the announced purposes of God. According to every indication, Jehovah's will is often the causative factor in these wars. Frequently He sanctioned, and sometimes even commanded, the utter annihilation of the enemy.

Already in the desert skirmishes the Lord had promised protection and support for His Chosen People. When the Hebrews were confronted with extreme peril, and the odds against them seemed overwhelming, the importunity of Moses resulted in a miraculous intervention and dramatic rescue. The pursuing army of the Egyptians drowned in the Red Sea while the Israelites walked through on dry land. In the song of triumph that commemorated their deliverance, the people sang: "The Lord is a warrior. . . . Pharoah's chariots and his army He cast into the sea. . . . It was Thy right hand, O Lord, that shattered the foe. By the greatness of Thy majesty Thou didst overthrow Thine adversaries; Thou didst loose Thy wrath, it consumed them like stubble" (Ex. 15:3ff). When the Amalekites challenged the passage of Israel at Raphidim, Joshua led the army against them while Moses, assisted by Aaran and Hur, implored Jehovah's help. Full victory was achieved and the Lord assured Moses: "I will blot out the very memory of Amalek from under the heavens" (Ex. 17:8–16). Shortly before Moses' death, the Lord expressly directed him "to execute the Lord's vengeance on Midian" (Num. 31:2ff).

After forty years of wandering in the Wilderness, the Israelites were commanded by God to enter Canaan and drive out or exterminate the inhabitants. They were told that their military campaigns would be divine missions. They were encouraged to be stalwart and brave because they would be fighting the Lord's battles. As Joshua stood before the walls of Jericho, he met a stranger with a drawn sword in his hand. This was the Angel of the Covenant, who gave him specific instructions from God for the demolition of the city.

Deborah the prophetess and Barak, the captain of the army, were directed by God in the battle against Sisera and the Canaanites. In her victory song Deborah exclaimed: "Curse Meroz, said the angel of the Lord, curse utterly its inhabitants; for they came not to the help of the Lord" (Judg. 5:23). During the first two days of battle with the Benjaminites, the rest of Israel suffered severe casualties, but Jehovah demanded that they persevere in the assault until the obdurate tribe was vanquished and its crime punished (Judg. 20:18ff).

Victory against the Philistines, on one occasion, was attributed to the fervent intercession of Samuel at Mispeh and the ensuing repentance of the people. "The Lord thundered with a mighty voice that day against the Philistines, and threw them into confusion and they were overcome before Israel" (I Sam. 7:10). When the witch at Endor called up the departed spirit of Samuel, Saul was reminded of the cause of his rejection: "Because you did not listen to the voice of the Lord, and did not execute the fierceness of His wrath against Amalek" (I Sam. 28:18).

After the surrounding tribes had been subdued and many invasions had been repulsed, God spoke to David through the prophet Nathan: "Thus says the Lord of hosts. . . . I have cut off all your enemies from before you" (II Sam. 7:9). In summarizing all the battles of the warrior-king, it is asserted: "Thus the Lord gave David victory wherever he went" (II Sam. 8:14b). Facing both a frontal and a rear attack from the Ammonites and the Syrians, Joab bolstered the morale of his army with a "pep talk": "Be courageous, and let us show ourselves strong for the sake of our people and for the cities of our God; and may the Lord do that which is good in His sight" (II Sam. 10:12).

In the victor's hymn of praise that is appended to the Second Book of Samuel, Jehovah is depicted as the Avenger of David's foes. The narrow escapes in the face of imminent peril, every *coup de maître,* and all acquisitions of subjugated territory are ascribed to the intervention of a favorably disposed Providence. Whenever calamity threatened and defeat seemed inevitable: "He let fly His arrows and scattered them, lightning, and discomfited them." David did not fear his antagonists, "for through Thee I can break down a rampart, through my God I can scale a wall." The Lord approved of David's military ventures. He was "the one who trains my hands for battle." "All hail to the Lord!" exclaimed David, ". . . the God who gives me vengeance." The Lord ignored the desperate cries of David's opponents, while "I grind them to powder like the dust of the earth, I crush them like the dirt of the streets by stamping upon them" (II Sam. 22).

In the following chapter, thirty-two heroes of war are listed and their exploits glorified. Honors were conferred upon Ishbaal because he "raised aloft his spear over eight hundred slain at one time." The valiance of Benaiah is acclaimed because he overcame a formidable-looking and well armed Egyptian.

In the Chronicles of the Kings, it is related that soon after David established his reign in Jerusalem he contemplated a sortie against the Philistines. But first he waited for divine endorsement. The assurance was forthcoming: "Go up, for I will deliver them into your hand." After the successful onslaught of his army, David gave full credit where it was due: "God has broken through my enemies by my hand, like the bursting water through a dam" (I Chron. 14:10–17).

The secession of the ten Northern tribes dissociated them from the benefits accruing to membership in the established realm. This illegal rupture broke their line of continuity with the Messianic promises. When civil war pitted Jews of the Southern Kingdom against their former countrymen of the North, divine favor rested with the "Loyalists." A cunningly contrived ambush failed to enmesh the warriors who had the Lord and the priests on their side. "God routed Jeroboam and all Israel before Abijah and Judah. . . . thus the Israelites were humbled at that time and the Judeans prevailed because they relied on the Lord, the God of their fathers" (II Chron. 13:15–18).

When Asa became king in the City of David, he removed the foreign altars and other evidences of idolatry. Not only was he personally righteous, but as a bold reformer he told his subjects to remember their covenant relationship with God and obey the Law. During a ten-year respite of quiet on the borders, he efficiently supervised the fortifying of the cities and the equipping of the army. An invasion by a million Ethiopians did not catch him unprepared. Besides, Asa was a pious king, and did not neglect to invoke the power of the Almighty. Before the battle he lifted his voice in fervent prayer:

O Lord, there is none besides Thee to help,
As between the mighty and him that is without strength.
Help us, O Lord, our God;
For we rely on Thee,
And in Thy name we have come against this multitude,

> O Lord, Thou art our God;
> Let not man prevail against Thee.

The outcome was overwhelming victory. The Ethiopian hordes were routed and fled in panic. Cities were captured and a rich plunder was enjoyed (cf. II Chron. 14).

"The terror of the Lord" prevented surrounding nations from making war against Jehosaphat. Because "he walked in the earlier ways of David his ancestor and did not seek the Baals," he was rewarded with wealth and prosperity (cf. II Chron. 17:10ff).[5] After numerous victories had repelled most of the traditional foes, "Then a terror from God came upon all the kingdoms of the countries when they heard that the Lord fought against the enemies of Israel" (II Chron. 20:29). Accordingly, when Uzziah campaigned against the Philistines and the Arabs, he gained the ascendancy because "God helped him" (II Chron. 26:7).

Some of the Psalms are songs of thanksgiving for triumph in battle. David clearly attributed his skill in war to the propitious dispensation of God. His praise is directed to "the God who girds me with might . . . the One who trains my hands for battle." His opponents might cry for help, but all to no avail. "Then I pulverize them like dust before the wind; I crush them like the dirt of the streets." Foreigners submitted to him because he wielded the invincible power of God.

> All hail to the Lord! And blessed be my Rock!
> And may the God of my deliverance be exalted!
> The God who gives me vengeance,
> And puts peoples in subjection under me;
> Who frees me from my foes.
> Yea, Thou dost exalt me above my adversaries;
> From violent men Thou dost rescue me.[6]

So the vexing problem still arises: How can Christians harmonize Old Testament militarism with their profession to be a peace-loving and peace-promoting people? Granted, some of the excesses and atrocities were contrary to God's will. Admittedly, not every battle or war was instigated by Jehovah. Yet many were. How is the Christian apologist to explain the dominating martial spirit of the Old Testament?

Undoubtedly, we will fall short of a completely satisfying answer. The inscrutable mysteries of God's judgments cannot be measured according to standards we have evolved. The sovereign Lord of the universe cannot be confined within categories of morality that we have set up. We are only the clay that He has fashioned into human form. We cannot pry into the mystery of His unsearchable decrees and His eternal purposes.

Why God selected Abraham to be the progenitor of the Hebrew people, why He promised the Patriarchs that in their Seed all the nations of the earth would be blessed, why He chose the Children of Jacob as His special people, may never be comprehensible to our obscured vision and limited reason. But the Old Testament centers around the fact that God did these very things. As the bearers of the Messianic mission, the Israelites were stamped with a singular character that distinguished them from all other nations. Their monotheism, their religious festivals, and their high moral code made them unique among neighboring tribes and kingdoms. By an act of His majestic will God denominated them as His select people. To them He promised the Land of Canaan as an inheritance. For their protection and benefit He sometimes suspended the normal course of nature. Through His prophet Moses He conveyed to them His inviolable commandments in written form. As a constant reminder of their peculiar status before God, the Israelites were obliged to follow an intricate and detailed system of religious ceremonies and rites. In all the history of the world, ancient or modern, there has been nothing to duplicate, or even approximate, this preeminence of the Hebrew people. They were the original branches in God's olive tree, and the Gentiles were grafted in only after the intended benefactors had rejected the salvation offered in Christ (cf. Rom. 11).

In view of Israel's God-appointed role as the harbinger and vehicle of redemption, the many wars of the Old Testament begin to take on a different meaning. The descendants of Abraham could claim, as no other people could, that they represented a divine purpose. As individuals they might fall short of fulfilling their obligations under the Covenant, but the cause they exemplified as a people was righteous. The religion bequeathed to them was the true and pure one. Whoever dared to interfere with them deserved to suffer the consequences of incurring divine wrath.

At the same time, it should be remembered that God's Chosen People were called upon to separate themselves from the rest of the world (cf. Ex. 33:16). Thy were required to practice the proper worship as attested in the Book of Leviticus. They were to avoid every contaminating contact with the heathen. They were told: "You must be holy to Me; for I, the Lord, am holy, and have separated you from other peoples to be mine" (Lev. 20:26).

Even so, God's election of this one nation was a result of His gracious dispensation, and not in keeping with their deserts. "It was not because you were the greatest of all people that the Lord set His heart on you and chose you . . . but it was because the Lord loved you, and would keep the oath that He swore to your fathers . . ." (Deut. 7:7–8).[7]

The "peace churches" have reminded us, however, that not all is blood and thunder in the Old Testament. Not all of the source material is congenial to the militaristic position. A pacifistic tone seems to be injected occasionally, and the role of the peace-maker is extolled.

When there was strife between the herdsmen of Abraham and Lot, the patriarch generously conceded the best grazing land to his nephew so that the quarrel might cease (Gen. 13:7–12). When the envious Philistines stopped the wells which Isaac had dug, he refused to be provoked into revenge, and succeeded in establishing a peaceful agreement with his enemies (Gen. 26:12–33). One of the Proverbs advocates kind treatment of the enemy and is quoted by Jesus and St. Paul in the New Testament (Prov. 25:2). When the Syrian army which was sent to Dothan to seize Elisha was stricken with blindness and was at the mercy of the king of Israel, the prophet not only recommended clemency, but directed that bread and water be set before the Syrian soldiers and that they be dismissed unharmed. One of the complaints which Isaiah registers against his countrymen is their blood guilt. They have wantonly destroyed human life (Isa. 1:15; 59:3,7–8). In Isaiah 13 we read that God threatens the desolation of Babylon, and in Isaiah 16 judgment is pronounced on Moab, but Israel is not commanded to take up the sword against the oppressors. Sennacherib's army was destroyed by the intervention of Jehovah, without Israel's striking a blow. (Isa. 37; II Kings 19). The return from the Babylonian Captivity and the resettlement of Judah were to be carried out peacefully.

The pacifist argument suggest that "in the times of their ignorance God may have winked at Israel's inferior moral performance." When Christ established the New Covenant, God's people were required to "walk in a newness of life in which warfare and strife can have no part." [8] God's will has not changed, but the clarity with which it was revealed has changed. Since the redemptive work of Christ on the Cross was completed, it is urged, we have a more compelling incentive for adopting the peace ethic. The people that walked in darkness no longer have an excuse for remaining in darkness, now that the Light is available. God expects more of Christians, among whom the Gospel reigns supreme, than He could among the Israelites, who had only a partial understanding of God.

If we ask why God permitted a lower standard of conduct under the Old Covenant, the pacifist Christian, who wants to accept the whole Bible and claim that it is without contradiction, points to the statement of Jesus concerning Mosaic divorce, "From the beginning it was not so" (Matt. 19:4–8). Evidence is adduced to try to show that it was God's original intention to conduct a peaceful penetration of the Land of Canaan under His immediate direction (Ex. 23:20–33). The disobedience of Israel brought disaster, however. The people lived on such a low moral and spiritual level that God's plan for a peaceful conquest of the Promised Land had to be abandoned. When the Lord saw that the people refused the higher standard of nonresistance, He commanded war.

Such solutions of the problem strike us as a little far-fetched, and they come precariously close to attributing a sort of double ethical standard to God. When Jeremiah is cast in the role of an Old Testament pacifist who was charged with treason and imprisoned for advocating nonresistance, we suspect that someone is overstating his case. [9]

Nevertheless we must agree that the wars of the Old Testament cannot be cited as conclusive evidence for the admissibility of Christian participation in modern warfare. We no longer can speak of a "nation under God," which has been ordained to fight for divinely specified goals. The United States cannot pretend to be a theocracy, as Israel was in the days of the Judges and the Kings.

What we can and ought to learn from the Old Testament records is that war is and has been employed as a method of moral rectification. God uses war as a punishment for national sins. When the Israelites became reprobate and apostate, hostile armies were permitted to harass them until they returned to the Lord in sackcloth and ashes. Contempt for the Law of God, avarice and unrighteousness, false ambition and pride are mentioned as reasons for such punitive action. (Cf. Lev. 26:56; I Kings 8:23; Amos 9:1f; Micah 2:1f; and Isa. 1:5–6). Isaiah clearly denominates Assyria as the rod of God's anger and the staff of His indignation against Israel. Jeremiah designates Nebuchadnezzar as God's instrument for subjugating the nations of his day, including Judah. Ezekiel, acting as the oracle of the Lord, insinuates that Jerusalem was overrun by the Gentiles because "they had scorned my ordinances, and did not follow my statutes" (Ezek. 20:16).

Another remarkable observation that we might make regarding the Old Testament is the lack of all glorification of war or of warriors within its pages. War is a grim and gory necessity which befalls man because of his incurable sinfulness. If possible, it should be avoided. David, the foremost soldier of them all, was denied the honor of building the Temple because his hands were stained with blood. In spite of the stern realism of the Old Testament, we should remember that war is still pictured there as a dreadful calamity.

2

~~~~~~~~~~~~~~~~~~~~~~~~~~~~~~~~~

Pacifism in the New Testament?

Just as the exponents of militarism have drawn heavily on Old Testament sources, so the advocates of pacifism have gone to the New Testament to bolster their case. The claim is frequently advanced that Jesus was a pacifist, or at least that He taught non-resistance. The love which our Lord exemplified and taught, it is maintained, is utterly incompatible with Christian participation in warfare. Here again the pertinent sections of Scripture should be carefully examined as a prerequisite for evaluating the reactions of various church groups to the Second World War and its aftermath.

If we expect to encounter unequivocal assertions by Christ or the Apostles either endorsing or condemning war, we are doomed to disappointment. When, in our investigation, we turn to the New Testament for guidance, we find little or nothing that deals directly with the problem of war and peace. A retired chaplain, endeavoring to defend the traditional position of the Lutheran Church in encouraging her sons to fight in loyal support of the government, has explained Christ's silence on this point as proof that God's will as revealed in the Old Testament was not to be superseded or controverted by the New.[1]

Non-pacifists usually make the most of those occasions on which Jesus did not appear so gentle and mild. They call our attention to the physical force exerted in cleansing the Temple. In an outburst of righteous indignation Christ drove out the money-changers, whose dishonest practices were contaminating the Temple which has been dedicated to the glory of God. Apparently, however, this was a rare exception in the life of the Savior, since none of the Gospels record that He used violent means under any other circumstances.

Some of the strongly worded statements of Jesus are then quoted to further the arguments against pacifism. The many times He met and berated the Scribes and Pharisees are usually mentioned, especially the scathing anathemas which labeled them "liars" and "hypocrites" and sons of the devil, relegated to perdition. Wherever the stern justice of God is stressed in the Parables, the militarist may assume that he has found grist for his mill. Did God not threaten destruction to those who had done evil, such as the wicked vine-dresser (Matt. 21:41)? In the Parable of the Pounds, the nobleman who represented God concluded: "But as for these enemies of mine, who did not want me to reign over them, bring them here and slay them before me" (Lu. 19:27).[2] In the familiar judgment scene Christ Himself sat as Judge and condemned His opponents to the eternal fire prepared for the devil and his cohorts (Matt. 25:41). Obviously these stories describe the exercise of God's justice in eternally punishing sin. How or why they should be adduced to sanction modern warfare is not at all clear.

One of the most popular texts used in defense of war is the declaration of Jesus: "Render therefore to Caesar the things that are Caesar's, and to God the things that are God's" (Matt. 22:21). This passage was pivotal in Augustine's approval of war. Here Jesus drew a line of demarcation between two spheres of authority. The obligations which are due to God are spiritual, and no secular government dare infringe upon this sacred realm. At the same time, there must be social and political control if anarchy is to be averted. Even though Caesar may be pagan, he has a right to impose taxation and require certain forms of service to the state.[3]

Often coupled with the statement of Jesus has been Paul's appeal to the Romans for subordination to the existing authorities (Rom. 13:1–4). The usual argument that follows is that "the powers that be" have a responsibility in maintaining a semblance of peace and outward conformity with law. To be effective, they must develop police protection and recruit military forces. It is difficult to see, though, how these verses can definitely settle the issue about whether or not a Christian ought to go to war. In themselves they contain no refutation of pacifism. They would still not allow the state to be independent of the God by Whose permission they rule. Divine law continues to be superior to temporal power. There is a limit to what the government can demand. It dare not go contrary to the higher law, which insists that "we are to obey God rather than man" (Acts 5:29). The problem remains whether or not Christian involvement in the rapacity and ruthlessness of war can be harmonized with the moral law and the interpretation provided by Christ and the Apostles.

Augustine claimed that early Christians who were soldiers were never directed to renounce their military profession before being accepted in the Church. It is true that the believing centurion was not reprimanded by Jesus for being a soldier. His ailing servant was healed without any reference to his occupation. Peter welcomed into the Christian fellowship another centurion, Cornelius, who was pronounced "a righteous man and one that feared God" (cf. Acts 10). Evidently there was no demand that he first abandon his position in the Roman army. When the soldiers were converted in the Jordan wilderness by the fiery preaching of John the Baptist, they inquired what they should do to display their newly experienced repentance. The reply seems to assume that they would remain soldiers after their baptism: "Rob no one by violence or by false accusation, and be content with your wages" (Lu. 3:14).[4] But again we find nothing conclusive in these instances which are so frequently cited. Defenders of slavery could argue, on the same grounds, that Jesus supported the domination of one class by another because He never required that masters free their slaves.

The use of our Lord's assertion, "Do not think that I have come to bring peace on earth; I have not come to bring peace, but a sword" (Matt. 10:34), is obviously based on a literal misinterpretation of what was intended to be a metaphorical expression. As the context shows, Jesus was stressing the self-sacrifice that would be necessary whenever anyone took his discipleship seriously. The cost of following Christ might even include the estrangement of family and friends. On this text we may read Schleiermacher with interest and approval: "His gentle soul could not possibly have meant that He was come to occasion those bloody commotions, so utterly contrary to the spirit of religion. But 'those holy wars . . . which . . . render hearts asunder.'" [5]

More disturbing to the pacifist outlook is the last discourse which Jesus had with His disciples, when He cautioned them to be prepared for future exigencies by equipping themselves with ample provisions, including swords (Lu. 22:35–38). The exact intent of our Lord's remarks is rather obscure. Some commentators suggest that He was recommending means of self-defense which would be indispensable during their later missionary journeys because of the physical perils they would face.[6] Other exegetes are inclined to think that Jesus was preparing them for the situation immediately at hand, namely, His arrest in Gethsemane.[7] At any rate, pacifist writers are quick to remind us that when Peter used his sword in the Garden he was rebuked and told that those who took the sword would perish by the sword.[8]

The martial symbols used in the Scriptures have been mentioned as evidence against pacifism. The Christian Church is often compared to an army following Jesus Christ as the invincible Commander. The Book of Revelation pictures Christ as a Warrior on a white horse leading His celestial legions to triumph in battle. John testifies that in his astounding vision he saw a sharp sword issue from His mouth, with which He would smite the nations. In bellicose terms he describes how "He will tread the wine press of the fury of the wrath of God the Almighty" (Rev. 19:11–16). Paul admonishes the Ephesians to put on "the whole armor of God," which includes "the breastplate of righteousness," "the shield of faith with which you can quench all the flaming darts of the evil one," "the helmet of salvation," and "the sword of the Spirit" (Eph. 6:13–17). Along with figures of speech taken from athletic contests, the Apostle makes comparisons between Christian witness and military life. He encourages his young friend Timothy to persevere in his hardships: "Take your share of suffering as a good soldier of Christ Jesus. No soldier on service gets entangled in civilian pursuits, since his aim is to satisfy the one who enlisted him" (II Tim. 2:3,4).

And yet, all this use of warlike imagery need not imply divine sanction of war. Evil is a reality in the life of the Christian, and the spiritual struggles in which he is involved are inescapable. It is no more than natural that Biblical writers should have sought to make these conflicts more vivid by using illustrations from the battle-ground of physical combat. At the same time, in criticism of the dogmatic pacifist, it would seem strange that all these allusions were made to war without a hint that the Christian must renounce all things military. The impression conveyed by the New Testament is that the stationing of Roman battalions in Palestine and the application of force by the prevailing authorities was something necessary to maintain the structure of society. The Christian was to be neither a revolutionist nor an anarchist. Jesus told Pilate that His Kingdom was not of this world. We cannot imagine Him leading the fanatical Zealots in an insurrection designed to overthrow the existing regime. Neither can we feature His recommending that the police power of the state be rescinded and disavowed. His Kingdom was a spiritual domain that brought people into a living relationship with God. Those who were committed to Him in faith and trust had "one foot in heaven." But the foot that remained on earth still had to reckon with "the kings of the Gentiles," comply with their laws, and offer them support. There is no intimation that Jesus expected that His followers would be able to evade the harsh realities of war in a corrupt and sinful world.

3

~~~~~~~~~~~~~~~~~~~~~~~~~~~~~~~~~~~

Christian Participation in World War II and Its Aftermath

A. THE LUTHERAN CHURCH

To evaluate correctly the Lutheran reaction to the question of participation in the Second World War and the Korean War, it is necessary to recall the position taken by Luther and the Lutheran Confessions. The Augsburg Confession declared: "It is right for Christians to bear civil office, to sit as judges, to judge matters by the Imperial and other existing laws, to award just punishments, to engage in just wars, to serve as soldiers. . . ."[1] The Apology refers to the wars of David as "holy works."[2] Private vengeance is forbidden but public redress is commanded. Among the ways in which public redress may be achieved are "legal decisions, capital punishment, wars, military service."[3]

One of the classical sources for the Lutheran attitude toward war is the Reformer's treatise defending the proposition *That Soldiers, Too, Can Be Saved.* The sum and substance of his thought is that force in itself is a divine and useful ordinance established by God. The occupation of the soldier is an honorable one. If the soldier performs his duty in obedience to the government, if he kills only as a last resort, and if he is prayerful and reverent even in the shedding of blood, he cannot be held responsible for his acts. However, if he destroys human life for the sheer joy of killing and holds hatred in his heart against his fellow man, he must be held accountable for transgressing against the Fifth Commandment. A soldier must have the proper motives. He dare not fight to attain personal glory. Then, too, he dare not violate his conscience and join in a war which would obviously be unprovoked aggression.[4] No one should instigate war. At the same time, no one should refuse to bear arms when required to do so for the defense of family and neighbors. If a person has ties binding him to both sides in a conflict, he must fight for the side which he believes to be right.[5]

Submission to the authorities ordained by God was mandatory in Luther's thinking on the problem of war. In his *Treatise Concerning the Ban* he averred: "God cannot and will not permit authority to be wantonly and impudently resisted when it does not force us to do what is against God or His commandments." [6] Referring primarily to ecclesiastical leaders who impose the ban unjustly, he recommended nonresistance. In the same connection he commented: "The world is far too wicked to be worthy of good and pious lords, it must have princes who go to war, levy taxes, and shed blood. . . ." [7]

Luther severely criticized the Council of Nicea because of its opposition to war. The decree forbidding Christians to perform military service on pain of seven years' penance proved to him the fallibility of Church councils:

> If a king or prince has to fight and defend himself in a just war, he has to take what soldiers he can get. But if these volunteers are condemned, what will become of emperors, kings and princes, now that there are no soldiers to be had except volunteers? Tell me, are the lords to fight single-handed, or weave strawmen to oppose their enemies?"

Luther was sure that the *milites* and *equites* in A.D. 325 were paid professional soldiers, and he inquired: "If it was right before Baptism to serve heathen emperors in war, why should it be wrong to render the same service to Christian emperors, after Baptism?" [8]

When the Holy League of Nürnberg appeared to threaten the Lutherans with war, Luther was of the cautiously conceived judgment that the Protestants could rightfully resist this alliance of princes. However, he warned the Smalcaldic League against waging a preventive war which would make them morally culpable. They must await some overt act of aggression by the Roman Catholic princes before striking back. After consulting with the jurists of Wittenberg, and being assured that they were on safe ground according to the laws of the empire, Luther and his fellow theologians, Jonas, Bugenhagen, Amsdorf, and Melanchton, agreed that a war of self-defense was permissible.[9]

In the Lutheran elucidation of what comprises a just war, frequent reference is made to the Lutheran dogmatician of the seventeenth century, John Gerhard.[10] Usually citations are limited to his enumeration of the three causes of a just war: necessary defense, just vindication, and the legitimate recovery of lost property.

It would make for a more balanced view if Gerhard were examined on *all* aspects of this problem. He warned, for example, against perpetrating war without due provocation: "When kings hear that right and just warfare is approved by God, let them by no means think that free rein is given to their cupidity, lust and passion, nor that the most unrestricted power of waging war is granted them." [11] He denied that recourse to arms was permissible in every case of defense. The circumstances must first be scrupulously examined.[12] He further cautioned against preventing a private grievance from instigating a war that would involve a whole region or state, "lest the innocent are made to expiate the guilt of others." [13] Pious and Christian rulers were to remember that they must render an account before God for the way in which they had exerted their authority. They were forbidden to embark recklessly on a course which would lead to needless bloodshed.

1. *The Lutheran Church—Missouri Synod*

In a tract entitled *War and Christianity*, Dr. Graebner, of the Concordia Seminary in St. Louis, quoted the pertinent paragraphs from the Lutheran Confessions, defended the distinction between a just and an unjust war, and insisted that Lutherans should render loyal and patriotic service in accord with Romans 13.[14] It was even conceivable, the professor asserted, that "the aggressor may have a good cause." Effective military strategy might compel the innocent nations to take the offensive. Sometimes, he admitted, the whole issue of war or peace might be confused by a complexity of causes. Then he recommended that the individual follow the advice of Luther and "give his own country the benefit of the doubt." Unless it could be unmistakably established that his government was pursuing a policy of deliberate and premeditated aggression, he had no justification for becoming a conscientious objector.

In 1941, before our country was directly involved in World War II, the Reverend Louis J. Roehm advised the young men with a doubting conscience to observe the common rule "*Tene certum, relinque incertum.*" If a person could not determine for himself what is right or wrong, he ought to relinquish what was dubious and take his stand on something certain. "Your government is instituted by God; therefore obey its mandate, and you can have a good conscience." Besides, he went on, the Church was scarcely in a position to make a valid pronouncement on the justice or injustice involved in a question of war or peace, because of the deceptive propaganda by which any such issue was beclouded. Not everyone had access to the archives of the government, which might reveal the underlying causes of a war which he was being called upon to support. So, Mr. Roehm concluded:

> A Christian pastor should therefore counsel and exhort his parishioners to pray for their government and be alert citizens; through the orderly processes of democratic government to make their voices heard in opposition to all measures they consider as militating against security, order, and righteousness; in time of national stress to uphold the government loyally and to resist only when commanded to sin.[15]

This position was reaffirmed throughout the war, and after the war, in church magazines and publications. The armed forces of a country were called its "police force." If a Christian could resist evil in civilian life by serving as an officer of the law, it was argued, he could also uphold order on a national and international scale by joining the Army or the Navy.[16]

Although admitting a measure of American responsibility for the oubreak of the war, Dr. O. A. Geiseman demanded that criminal actions like that evinced at Pearl Harbor be restrained.[17] The government should wield the sword as speedily and effectively as possible, he argued. Along the troubled horizon he saw a "silver lining," for the war had unified the nation. It might have other beneficial results. It might pave the way for future international agreements by showing the need for them. It might cause men to experience the futility of their vain ambitions, and turn to Christianity.

Sermons printed by the Armed Services Commission of The Lutheran Church—Missouri Synod sometimes tended to identify the Allied cause with the righteousness of God and the Axis powers with Satanic evil. The definite claim was made that God was on our side. In a V-E Day sermon the Reverend F. C. Proehl compared our victory over Germany and Japan to Jacob's deliverance from his brother Esau. "We have become strong in this business of war and carried the war to the very strongholds of the enemy. The Lord has blessed our efforts. He has given success to our arms. . . ." Miriam's song of triumph over the drowning of Pharoah's hosts was applied to the Allied victory in Europe. Gratitude was expresssed for the sparing of our cities from the ravages of war. "For the sake of the righteous, God has preserved our cities and kept them from harm." [18]

In a sermon based on the account of Israel's battle with the Amalekites (Ex. 17:8–13), Dr. Louis B. Buchheimer attempted to reassure disturbed young minds: "Let none of you doubt the scripturalness of bearing arms in our country's defense. . . . our soldiers and sailors are wielding 'the sword' for our government, for us. We must make the sword as keen as possible." [79] Just as Sennacherib's army was smitten by an angel of the Lord in the days of Hezekiah, so in modern times the Spanish Armada had been destroyed "by a God-sent storm." The English army had contrived a remarkable escape from Dunkerque after the debacle in France because God had provided a dense fog and made the English Channel extraordinarily calm.

August F. Bernthal compared the Christian soldier's call to duty with God's call to Abram to leave his homeland and become the progenitor of a great nation. "Our country's call to the Christian soldier is God's call." All of the promises regarding God's providential care and protection could be applied to the Christian soldier in his loneliness and peril.[20]

In the orders of service prescribed for the day when hostilities would cease, victory was always to be ascribed to Almighty God's intervention in our behalf. "Great is the victory Thou hast given to our Nation and to our Allies" was the pronouncement in one recommended prayer.[21] A sermon published for use with the V-Day Thanksgiving service devoted an entire section to "God, the Giver of Victory." There were "imponderable factors which only God can know and control." Why had Germany and Japan been unable to follow through on their initial successes? What had prevented Rommel from marching on Alexandria? The implication was that God was on *our* side, and not on *theirs*.[22]

A special song was composed in honor of the armed forces of our nation by Walter E. Buszin. It sounded a martial note:

> Fear not the foe, ye men of war,
> Strong in the power of Almighty God;
> Courage maintain, on, on, and fight,
> Our cause is just, our faith is strong.
> Forward to battle, win this war,
> God be your Shield, He's e'er by your side.
>
> Fear not the foe, ye sons of peace,
> Think of the outcome, ponder the end;
> Forward to vict'ry, let freedom ring,
> Loud songs of triumph sing with glee.
> O God in heaven, hear our prayer,
> Help those who battle, grant them Thy care.[23]

With favorable editorial comment *The Lutheran Chaplain* printed a statement by General Dobbie, former Governor of Malta, in which he confessed his reliance upon Biblical truth. Then the editor appended this thought:

> When we compare this type of leadership with that which has guided Germany during the past era, we thank God that our allies are motivated by the Spirit of Christ in their

dealings with the enemy and that they cannot become ruthless in their conduct over against him. Our warfare is tempered with compassion and love. Thank God for this type of leadership! [24]

In the light of subsequent disclosures of Allied brutality and vengeance, the admitted maltreatment of war prisoners, and the use of "saturation bombing" as an accepted method of warfare, these sentiments would strike many as reflections of a naïve chauvinism.

Pastors serving Lutheran students at state universities during the war years reported that there was considerable criticism of the traditional concept of a just war. To some students it seemed like an oversimplification of an intricate problem. Many expressed their misgivings about the righteousness of our cause. Questions like these were raised: "How can we say that one side is a hundred percent right and the other a hundred percent wrong?" "Doesn't our own country participate in the game of power politics?" "Isn't our government employing pressure devices, such as economic sanctions?" "Don't these tactics indirectly urge a rival nation to declare war on us?" Admittedly, it was difficult to provide adequate answers in line with the historic Lutheran approach.[25]

Church editors occasionally ventured opinions that had to be retracted or revised when the war was over. Expediency made strange alliances. Before the outbreak of the war *The Cresset* called Stalin "the prince of the devils" and warned against being misled by pro-Russian propaganda.[26] The Russian invasion of defenseless Finland was called "unprovoked aggression" and compared to the seizure of Naboth's vineyard by King Ahab.[27] But after the German invasion of the Lowlands, criticism of Soviet Russia was conspicuously omitted, while no condemnation was too severe for the Nazi "barbarism" which was running rampant in Europe. Attacking peaceful neutrals like Denmark and Norway was "a moral wrong of the most infamous kind." [28] Apparently there was little or no concern any longer about the fate of Eastern Poland and the Baltic countries that were under the iron heel of Russian oppression. An editorial in the official publication of the Missouri Synod intimated that Soviet Russia had changed its colors. What was once reprehensible about the Soviet system had in all likelihood been eliminated. The charges of atheism and ruthlessness once associated with the Bolshevik Revolution in 1917 were dismissed as outmoded. As evidence, the editor pointed to the dismemberment of the Third International and its official disavowal by the Kremlin. The reopening of the churches in Germany by the Russians presumably indicated a new tolerance toward religion. It would be particularly embarrassing today to recall the same writer's appraisal of the Chinese situation in 1945:

> The Russian armies did not make common cause with the Chinese Communists as everybody expected, but with the government in Chungking, and they promised to give up Manchuria and make a thirty-year treaty of peace with China. Where are the Bolshevik hordes which some of us saw rolling across China and engulfing in Red Communism all of Asia? [29]

With bitter irony, an observer in 1952 would have given an altogether different answer from the rhetorical question anticipated, by bluntly exclaiming: "Killing American soldiers and ravaging the Korean peninsula." (In 1956 he might have added, "Menacing Formosa and posited as a constant threat to Japan, the Philippines, and the East Indies.") And so, two years later, the same editor had to reverse his judgment and admit:

> Soviet Russia has capitalized fully upon the disorganization and chaos in this area, exactly as she has done in Europe. Soviet propaganda and Soviet support of the Chinese Communist movement have increased the difficulty of establishing order in China. [30]

The threat of Communism belittled during the war was gradually revealed after 1946, so that even the unwary, who had hitherto been duped by the propaganda emanating from Moscow, could no longer shut their eyes to its fateful import.

The sudden death of Franklin Delano Roosevelt excited some curious and almost adulatory eulogies. Some congregations arranged special memorial services. A Missouri Synod ministerial-preparatory college conducted devotions in his honor and pronounced him a great man. [31] Even the publication for Spanish

Lutherans took notice of his passing and was confident that he had been a faithful Christian.[32] Dr. O. A. Geiseman expressed his conviction that the magnitude of Roosevelt's achievements was founded on his passionate adherence to "the promises of God and the ethical principles of Christ." All the world, he was certain, could be transformed if "all who profess Christianity were to give a similarly genuine expression to their faith."[33] In a sermon preached in Baltimore, the Reverend Rudolph Ressmeyer lamented the untimely decease of the President, which would prevent his appearance at the peace table. "It reminds us," he opined, "of Moses not reaching the Promised Land."[34] One wonders if this saintly halo has not been tarnished by the publication of the Yalta papers. We can only conjecture as to how many memorial services might have been cancelled if the officiating ministers had heard of Roosevelt's proposal to Stalin that a toast be drunk to the killing of fifty thousand German officers.

To the credit of many church leaders in the Missouri Synod, it should be mentioned that they made a concerted effort to warn against a spirit of vengeance, and tried to prepare their members for a humble acceptance of victory. Aware that "the majority of our people will again refuse to recognize that our victory is an act of divine grace," they urged all pastors to be prepared with appropriate services which would express full gratitude to God.[35]

Some preachers during the war did not shrink from castigating Americans for their national sins and reminding their hearers that the war was a call to heartfelt repentance.

Outstanding was the clarion voice of Dr. Walter A. Maier, renowned radio orator on the International Lutheran Hour broadcast. Like a modern Jeremiah, he lamented the waywardness of the American nation and the apostasy of many Christians. With poignant accusations he enumerated and denounced the favorite sins of the people. Racial intolerance, divorce and moral laxity, greed and corruption in high places were singled out as causes of American decadence.[36] Military defense, he asserted, could never become a substitute for spiritual defense. "On your knees, America!" was his continual plea for revival and reformation.

During the months and years preceding our active entrance into the war, Dr. Maier indicted the false propaganda and profiteering that were pushing us down the road toward belligerency. He warned against the scheming forces that were endeavoring to maneuver us away from our neutrality. Frequently he bemoaned the increasing hysteria that threatened to stampede us into the European conflict. Fervent prayers for peace were preliminary to many of his sermons. With all the influence that he could exert over the airways, he sought to prevent the collapse of peaceful negotiations.

When hostilities came, there was never the slightest hint of disloyalty in his attitude, however. The youth of the land were encouraged to make every sacrifice necessary in support of the armed forces. But the Lutheran Hour speaker always maintained a moderate tone in his advocacy of patriotism. There was no let-up in his insistence that "only righteousness exalts a nation." Our involvement in war and all the attendant suffering were our due punishments for outright unbelief or, at least, widespread indifference to the truth of God's Word.[37]

While vicious outbursts of hatred against the enemy came from many quarters, Dr. Maier spoke of how we must emulate the merciful forgiveness displayed by Christ on the Cross. A proposal by a New York psychiatrist to keep fanning the fires of hatred to ensure German and Japanese suppression after the war was rejected as "utterly absurd." With all our aversion toward the evils of Nazism, Dr. Maier declared, "we dare not . . . permit our hearts to be filled with bitterness and malice toward the German people." [38]

Editors of Sunday school literature advised teachers to put "the soft pedal" on the subject of war and avoid its brutalizing aspects. Nothing should be said which might engender hatred against our enemies. Children should be taught to pray for the Christianization of Japan. True patriotism should be depicted as contributing to "the righteousness that exalts a nation," and not in blatant boasting about American military might. Having been drawn into the conflict, we should recognize it as "a just visitation of Heaven," censuring and punishing us for our drift toward paganism.[39]

During the Korean War there was no discernible change in the official outlook of this church body. Its leaders carefully refrained from any criticism of the decision to "halt the aggression in Korea."

This warfare was again recognized as "a scourge which God uses under His control and for His own purposes to chastise the world and bring it to its senses." Prayer for peace was recommended, but with the realization that peace would never be fully attained in this life.[40] Our tax money was helping to pay for "God's ministry of the sword to preserve that peace through which the ministry of the Word may be unhindered." [41]

Without disavowing in any way the usual Lutheran willingness to follow the government in conducting a just war, this denomination has exhibited a greater ethical sensitivity in recent years. An effort was made in 1950, however feebly, to interpret the role of the Christian fighting under the banner of his own country and the United Nations: "This war means that the American Christian professes to love people, and the cause of their freedom, who live on the other side of the globe." [32] Quiescent conformity with whatever happened was no longer sufficient, it was maintained. Praying was not enough. Christians were urged to find out what was endangering the peace, and, upon discovering the cause, to seek to remedy it. "Learning what needs to be done and then doing it all adds up to the Psalmist's admonition: 'Depart from evil and do good; seek peace and pursue it.'" [43]

Interestingly enough, the brutalizing aspects of the war in Korea were deplored in an editorial, whereas Hiroshima and Dresden had never evoked a syllable of regret. The churchmen were concerned because dispatches from the war front stressed with some satisfaction the fact that for every American life lost, a much larger number of North Koreans were being killed. Instead of conserving life where possible, our troops were being ordered to kill as many of the enemy as possible. The hope was expressed

> that the leaven of Christianity in the world will keep at a minimum the useless slaughter of human beings endowed with precious souls, especially where these souls are not prepared to meet their God. No Christian can without deep emotion read of these misguided heathen from North Korea being dispatched to their eternal doom, largely by nations who profess Christianity. The slogan of Christ's disciples was not "kill, kill!" but "save, save!" [44]

An editorial in *The Cresset* predicted that another world war would be suicidal folly. The only hope to which we could cling would be mere survival, and it was to be doubted that this would be a sufficient motive for going to war. Besides, we were apt to take on the undesirable characteristics of our enemies:

> It would be sheer tragedy if, in fighting Communism, we created within Western society the very conditions upon which Communism thrives; if in the battle to destroy authoritarianism, we became ourselves the victims of it. . . . We pray God save us (Russians and Yugoslavs, Syngman Rhee, Mao Tse-tung) from ourselves.[45]

In retrospect, it would appear that there have been some misgivings among American Christians about the Korean venture. Although there seems to have been no alternative to intervention, the fear has been expressed that the Asiatic countries which are still hovering between East and West may not see any purpose in the stalemate and may blame the United States for the devastated countryside and the shattered cities.[46]

While the condemnation of Nazism by the churches was categorical, and the call for victory over the Axis powers was unqualified, in the struggle with Communism there seems to have been a sudden awakening to the limited righteousness of our cause. The choice which the Christian must now make is represented as that between two evils. The Christian should not give unstinted support, however, to either the militaristic or the pacifistic position. The President of the University of Tampa is patently wrong when he advocates "total preparedness based on the laws of the jungle" and approves the use of bacteriological and atomic warfare. But neither will a refusal to take up arms at all fulfill the Christian's responsibility. The man of God fights hard and well, all the while knowing that he is involved in an evil which he has accepted in preference to a greater evil, "and he finds in the all-sufficiency of his Savior's merit an atonement for his evil. And beyond that he fights without hatred of those whom circumstances have made the object of his fighting and with the hope that both he and those whom he fights will benefit from the fruits of victory.[47]

Strangely enough, now that the ideological conflict is much more clear than it was during the Second World War, and a crusade against anti-Christian forces would have much more to commend it, the issue does not appear as clear-cut to Lutherans as it did from 1939 to 1945. Now the Church must be warned against "the temptation to equate the national will with the Divine Will." Now we can be told that we should resist any attempt "to convert Christianity into an American Shintoism." [48]

At its national convention in Houston, Texas, in June 1953, a memorial requesting that the synod declare its position regarding conscientious objection in time of war was submitted and then withdrawn. None the less, rumblings of dissatisfaction with the official position of the Lutheran Church-Missouri Synod on war may have evoked a subsequent resolution "to direct a theologian of our Church to prepare a clear and concise statement on 'A Christian's Attitude Towards War." [49]

In response to this resolution, the following theses (among others) were presented by Dr. L. W. Spitz of the Concordia Seminary in St. Louis and printed in the official theological journal of the church:

* * * *

4. God does not condemn the profession of a soldier, but concedes to the government the power of the sword. At the same time, however, He blesses the peacemakers. Accordingly a Christian prays for his government, personally works to maintain peace, and opposes the demonic forces which cause wars.

5. Although a Christian recognizes the right of the government to call him to arms in a just war, he does not concede that right to the government in an unjust war. In view of the complex nature of modern international affairs, it is extremely difficult for a citizen who is not acquainted with all the factors which may lead his country into a war to determine whether or not a specific war is a just war. This difficulty also holds true for members of the church who are not acquainted with the international problems of their government. Therefore the question whether in a specific case the government is waging

a just or an unjust war is usually not for the church to determine, but must be referred to the judgment of the individual.

6. A Christian who believes that God has given the government the power of the sword is not a pacifist; but if anyone is convinced in his own mind either that the use of military force for any purpose whatever is wrong or that a specific war is not a just war, he must refuse to bear arms, for he must not violate the dictates of his conscience. If he is not certain, he should give his government the benefit of the doubt, since God, who has instituted the government, will hold it responsible for its acts.

* * * *

8. In conclusion, inasmuch as the question of war has disturbed the conscience of some of the members of the church in the past and, in view of the character of modern warfare, may do so again to an even larger extent, our church should concern itself with the wider aspects of the problems involved and encourage its members, both individually and collectively, to study them. Above all, may our church continue to pray God to preserve us from war and bloodshed.[50]

* * * *

2. *The United Lutheran Church*

While the Lutheran Church—Missouri Synod, in its official publications and declarations, never deviated from its insistence that loyalty to government was the paramount consideration and that our participation in the Second World War was fully justified, the United Lutheran Church allowed for a greater latitude of variant opinion. Pacifist sentiments were not barred from the pages of *The Lutheran*, and the right of conscientious objectors to full tolerance was maintained. Just prior to Pearl Harbor the entire case for pacifism was presented in a series of articles by Herbert T. Weiskotten, and the counter-arguments by T. A. Kantonen.[51]

Shortly after the outbreak of war in Europe, Dr. Traver affirmed: "The Church must speak out for peace in the name of God." The Spirit of Christ, he insisted, could not be reconciled with "the wholesale murder we call war." As a method of settling international disputes, war must be renounced because it recompensed evil for evil. No Christian could subscribe to the principle that "the end justifies the means" or "of two evils choose the lesser." [52]

Almost simultaneously a Canadian minister contended that "England is right in this war, and that she is fighting a just war, perhaps one of the most just in her long history." Even the Church had a stake in the outcome, he asseverated. Should the opposition emerge triumphant, Christianity might be suppressed. "The Church in Canada is praying that victory may be assured for the forces of right." [53]

A statement released by the U.L.C.A. Board of Social Missions, on January 17, 1940, pleaded for a restudy and reinterpretation of the stand taken by the Lutheran Confessions in regard to war. Unwilling to propose that war is *per se* evil, the authors of this statement felt uncomfortable because so many conscientious and careful reviews of the teachings of Jesus indicated that it was. With clarity and emphasis they expressed their belief that it was the obligation of the Church to stand resolutely against recourse to war and "admit the inviolability of the individual conscience in its attitude toward war." [54]

The executive board of the U.L.C.A. gave painstaking consideration to the plight of the conscientious objector, which was viewed with sympathy, if not approval, in some quarters. The interpretation of the Board allowed that although "it is the duty of the Christian citizen to bear arms and offer his life if need be in defense of his country . . . the individual right to conscientious objection is recognized." The Church might not approve of this stand, the Board continued, but it should safeguard the person who felt conscience-bound not to take up arms. As a practical aid to the government, it was recommended that the Church record the names of those among its members who were approved as *bone fide* C.O.'s. The absolute pacifist position was decried as inconsistent, as it "would seem to call for dissociation from citizenship." If necessary, the C.O. must be willing to stand alone and take the disciplinary consequences which might be incurred. A refusal to defend righteousness, the Board continued, was a denial of Christian love. No attempt was made to judge where righteousness was represented in the contemporary struggle in Europe.[55]

A number of pastors in the United Lutheran Church disagreed with the supposition that the C.O.'s position was morally questionable or inferior to that of the soldier who accepted military duty. One rejoinder demanded that a pastoral ministry be provided for those opposed to war, with the understanding that their course of action might prove to be the wisest, and that the Church should not permit them to be subjected to any indignities or disabilities other than those imposed on other citizens during wartime. Another minister argued that the Sixteenth Article of the Augsburg Confession required modification in the light of modern scientific development. In the future, he said, we might have to think in terms of an international authority which was not envisioned by the sixteenth-century reformers. Still another wrote that the Church should vigorously denounce the civil powers for constantly resorting to an unchristian method of righting wrongs.[56] At the Omaha convention of the U.L.C.A. in 1940, a resolution was offered giving the C.O. official approval along with the person who served in a military capacity, but it was voted down.[57]

The Reverend C. C. Georgi re-examined the attitude of Luther toward war and concluded that he could not be used with such facility as a patron of our modern wars. In Luther's estimation, even a defensive war wrought devastating havoc on the citizenry. That no Christian could really fight in a war as a Christian, he maintained, was clear from three facts: "1. It is against the command of Christ. 2. It hurts the Church. 3. Civilization is nowhere Christian. . . ."[58]

On March 5, 1941, President Knubel formulated a proclamation entitled "Christian Realism As to War":

> It seems to be quite true that a drift towards war for the United States has long been going on and steadily increases in strength. One senses the existence of a seeming conspiracy, or a planned desire, for war. One can almost name the groups of various characters which have been pressing for the attainment of war as an end. . . . The United States has been going farther and farther on this

path and perhaps the nation has gone too far to stop "short of war." When men and nations go too far, God permits them to have their way in order that ultimately His purposes may be carried out.

Another controversy concerned with Lutheran reactions to the war came to the foreground when a pastor questioned the propriety of one of the prayers used in the Army and Navy Service Book: "O Lord God of our Salvation, we beseech Thee to go forth with our Army, Navy, Air Forces, and by Thy right hand and Thy mighty arm gain for them the victory." [59] It was stigmatized as contrary to the Sermon on the Mount and Christ's spirit of forgiveness. Dr. Fischer defended its use with the allegation that a Christian might be able to fight with a good conscience. The individual soldier could not be charged with "personal guilt" for his actions. Whatever the Christian prayed for must be conditional, he concluded, because there was no absolute justice in human relations. [60]

After the Pearl Harbor attack, there was editorial silence in *The Lutheran* on the question of the morality of involvement in the world conflict. Lutheran co-operation with the war effort seemed to be assumed. People were asked to plan and search for peace. Mother's Day collections were sponsored for the support of service centers. The chaplaincy was called a necessary ministry. Beneficial results were foreseen: Military service was said to teach co-operation and increase respect for other denominations. Pastors who served would gain a renewed appreciation of missionary endeavor. Through varied contacts and constructive criticism, Lutherans would learn how to improve their liturgy and services. [61]

A National Lutheran Council bulletin, released on July 10, 1942, revealed a sincere attempt to define the relationship between the Church and a world at war:

1. We call all people to repentance and a rededication of their lives to the will of God.
2. We call upon our people in particular, and all Christian people in general, to dedicate themselves wholly, with every resource of heart and mind and conscience, to the defeat and destruction of this evil. We call upon our own people to give to our country the fullest meas-

ure of devotion and support, as the privilege and duty of Christian citizens.

3. We summon our people to an earnest, searching study of the ways and means to an enduring world peace.

4. If enduring peace is to come to mankind it can come only to men and through men who are wholly dedicated, through faith in Christ, and by the power of His Holy Spirit, to righteousness and good will.

5. [Warns Christians against the passions of hate and revenge.]

6. [Calls for a generous support of relief programs.]

7. [Advises that we seize the opportunity presented for world missions.]

8. The paramount service the Church has to render to a world at war is to proclaim the redemptive love of God, and to make men, indeed, the sons of God by the power of His Holy Spirit.

B. THE ROMAN CATHOLIC CHURCH

To understand the reaction of the Roman Catholic Church in America to the Second World War and the Korean War, it will be helpful to scan the position of the early Church Fathers and trace briefly the origin of the concept of a just war.[62]

Although the evidence is scanty for the first one hundred and fifty years of the Christian era, it appears that the early Church Fathers were opposed to participation in war. Celsus, an early literary opponent of Christianity, reproached Christians for being unpatriotic and refusing military service to the Emperor.[63] Justin Martyr, an ardent defender of the faith in the second century, took Isaiah's prophecy literally that swords would be beaten into ploughshares and spears into pruning hooks, and said that the followers of Christ would gladly go to death for His sake, but they would refrain from making war on their enemies.[64] The canons of Hippolytus in the early second century allowed Christians to remain in the army as long as their required duties did not entail the shedding of blood. But "a soldier of the civil authority must be taught not to kill men and to refuse to do so if he is condemned."[65] Origen disposed of the Old Testament wars with an allegorical interpretation, and took an absolute stand against the use of force: "We do not serve as soldiers under the Emperor, even though he require it." [66] Likewise, Tertullian and Cyprian repudiated war with outspoken disapprobation. At times Marcion appeared to advocate a holiness type of pacifism which feared defilement from the world. Then again he directed his invective against the vindictiveness of the God of the Old Testament. Always he insisted that the Cross was designed to save men, and would not allow them to destroy one another in war.[67] As late as 374, Basil the Great recommended that those who were required to kill in war should abstain from Communion for three years.[68]

But during the reign of Marcus Aurelius it was already reported that Christians were marching under the Emperor's banner. The Council of Arles in 314 proclaimed that "they who throw away their weapons in time of peace shall be excommunicate." [69] With the conversion of Constantine and his official adoption of the Christian religion, the tide turned completely. Later theologians, enjoying the protection and favor of the state, began to justify Christian collaboration in war. Athanasius (c. 350), known as the "father of orthodoxy," concluded: "Murder is not permitted, but to kill one's adversary in war is both lawful and praiseworthy." [70] Ambrose (c. 375) professed: "And that courage which either protects the homeland against barbarians, in war, or defends the weak at home, or saves one's comrades from brigands, is full of righteousness." [71] Living at the time of the barbarian invasions, Augustine looked upon war as the defense of a peace-loving state against plundering aggressors. Together with Ambrose he gave the first fully elaborated formulation of the theory of a *justum bellum*.

Gradually this developed into the classical Roman Catholic doctrine of "permissive war." Reference was made to it by Roman Catholic apologists in an attempt to determine what stand the Church should take on the Second World War. Active Christian support of war, according to this doctrine, is said to be justifiable: 1) when there is no doubt but that one side is right and the other wrong; 2) when the means for peaceful arbitration have been exhausted; 3) when there is a clear chance for success; 4) when the war is waged with civilized weapons; 5) when it remains a war between armed troops, and not against helpless civilians; and 6) when such evils as the murder of noncombatants and the violation of women have been banished.[72]

Due to the variance among the Church Fathers and difficulty in harmonizing all the papal encyclicals on the subject, the Church allowed a considerable latitude of opinion among its scholars and leaders in their reactions to World War II. Conscientious objectors were neither categorically condemned nor openly encouraged. The Catholic Association for International Peace, founded in 1926, which had long pleaded for the reduction of armaments, printed a leaflet, after hostilities had commenced in Europe, which commended a refusal to bear arms.[73]

After we had entered the war, there were still Catholic youths who went to C.O. camps. They quoted statements made by some of the popes in their defense, such as that of Pius XII: "Nothing is lost with peace; all may be lost with war." [74] Paul L. Blakely countered the arguments of C.O.'s and warned that if they trusted their own conscience alone they were guilty of following a Protestant principle to the extreme. Nevertheless, he conceded: "I have no objection to Catholic conscientious objectors." [75]

During the months of "the great debate" between "interventionists" and "isolationists," there was extensive vocal and literary opposition in Roman Catholic circles to our entrance into the war. Not all their spokesmen were as bombastic and obstreperous as the Detroit radio priest, Father Coughlin, who launched trenchant verbal blasts against the Administration over the airways. Yet there was widespread resistance to the drift toward war. In the fall of 1939, James M. Gillis expressed his loathing for Nazism together with his mistrust of England. There was such an admixture of right and wrong on both sides, he complained, that the only reasonable, moral stand for Americans to take was to remain aloof.[76] Early in 1940, James McCawley censured the churchmen who were beginning to beat the drums for war.[77] A Roman Catholic editor regretted that Jacques Maritain was pronouncing the war "just." John P. Delaney inquired: "Why do *we* fight in *their* war?" Our neutrality, he predicted, might be the only means of salvaging world civilization.[78] John LaFarge admitted his sympathy for the

Allied cause, but doubted that American intervention would achieve the desired result. Our interference might well compromise our principles, he asserted. We would be called upon to defend English capitalism and safeguard French colonial policy.[79] Daniel M. O'Connell warned that the steps leading to war should be critically scrutinized and resisted. If we became engulfed in this European tragedy, he argued, it would only produce another Versailles Treaty, with its vicious aftermath.[80] Paul L. Blakely controverted the arguments that moral obligations or legal commitments should induce us to manufacture armaments for England. We would not be justified in taking the initiative against Germany and Italy. "All will be lost by war," he warned.[81]

As late as December 1941 the *Catholic World* still presented and upheld the isolationists' position, and even after Pearl Harbor this publication regretted the course of action our government had pursued.[82] After the cessation of hostilities the Administration was blamed openly in its pages for the debacle at Pearl Harbor.[83] A satirical jibe entitled "Intervention Begins to Pay Off" insinuated that with trouble brewing in Palestine, Iran, and Indonesia, and a war raging in China, "we are in a pretty kettle of fish."[84]

Generally speaking, though, Roman Catholics, like most other Americans, accepted Pearl Harbor as an irrefutable verdict in the interventionist controversy, and as a clarion call to a united war effort. With some reluctance the editor of *The Catholic World* called the conflict in the Pacific a "duty we cannot dodge." It was wise and praiseworthy to "beware of entrance to a quarrel," but once we were in, we had to accept the reality of a deplorable situation.

The Jesuit weekly was quick to announce full support for our government after the Japanese had launched their attack. "In accordance with its consistent and traditional policy of sound Catholicism and sane Americanism," the editors promised to use every resource at their command to bring about "a speedy termination of war through the defeat of the enemy powers." Although not endorsing it as a holy war or religious crusade, they did esteem it "a struggle between the established Christian order and the revolutionary order of Fascism, Nazism and Marxism."[85] In 1945 the terms for unconditional surrender that were being offered to a desperate Japan were evaluated as "severe but hopeful." Admittedly these terms constituted an ultimatum, because the only alternative to capitulation was utter destruction, but supposedly the stringency of the terms was mitigated by the prospect of "a new order of peace, security, and justice."[86]

Not all Roman Catholic theologians and commentators were content to accept the popular dictum that "all's fair in love and war." Major George Fielding Eliot was rebuked for asking the United States to turn a deaf ear to any appeal to send food to those who might starve in the conquered countries during the winter of 1940–41, because it would ruin the effectiveness of the British blockade. "Granted the war—must they starve?" inquired Jerome P. Holland. Could we call ourselves Christians and harden our hearts to the cry of the hungry? Must we assume that Almighty God would "reward our charity by permitting a strengthened Hitler to destroy us?"[87]

The morality of "obliteration bombing" was critically examined by John C. Ford. This was defined as strategic bombing, by means of incendiaries and explosives, in which the target to be wiped out is a large area of a whole city, including residential districts. Not all the inhabitants of an enemy country—men, women, and children —could be regarded as legitimate objects of direct attack, the writer maintained. Obliteration bombing, he continued,

> is an immoral attack on the rights of the innocent. It includes a direct intent to do them injury. Even if this were not true, it would still be immoral, because no proportionate cause could justify the evil done; and to make it legitimate would soon lead the world to the immoral barbarity of total war. The voice of the Pope and the fundamental laws of the charity of Christ confirm this condemnation.[88]

The Commonweal carried an approved article by Norman Thomas in which he deplored the exaltation of mass destruction and the degrading influence that it was having on our own people. That atrocities were not limited to the Japanese, he said, was established by the recurrent accounts of our own soldiers about

American brutalities against the enemy. Particularly shocking to him was the hate campaign directed against the Japanese as a sub-human species. A sadistic short film, he revealed, was being sponsored and circulated by our War Department, entitled "Have You Killed a Jap?" [89]

Roman Catholic editors fell in line with the papal condemnation of American use of the atom bomb against Hiroshima and Nagasaki. One indignant reaction did not hesitate to record:

> I here and now declare that I think the use of the atomic bomb, in the circumstances, was atrocious and abominable, and that civilized people should reprobate and anathematize the horrible deed.

Phelps Adams was quoted from *The New York Sun* as reporting that he noticed little real rejoicing over the bomb among the people. Rather, he detected a "sense of oppression" and "shame-facedness" that might denote qualms of conscience.[90]

The war crime trials in Nuremberg were greeted with dubious misgivings in the Roman Catholic press. Melanie Stark outlined the proposals of Justice Jackson as in conformity with "the organic, though painfully slow, growth of international law." But, he admitted, "it is not easy to be victorious in the name of justice." [91] Percy Winner compared our role in the war trials to that of a high priest arrayed in Caesar's robes, and was not surprised that many consciences were ill at ease. In his estimation,

> it was a posthumous triumph for Hitler that we should have needed to go beyond the rule of existing law to try him. It was a tragic defeat for viable reason that we should have needed to improvise a new fantasy of spiritual virtue to unmake Hitler's evil fantasy.[92]

Throughout the conflict the interests of the Roman curia were always carefully safeguarded. No doubt the position taken by the highest ecclesiastical authority helped to shape Roman Catholic attitudes. Soon after the invasion of Poland, the Pope offered to serve as mediator in negotiating a "Roman peace." While others were fighting, the Vatican was "busy with constructive plans." The

Supreme Pontiff, who commanded the allegiance of twenty million Americans as well as nearly forty million Catholics under the control of Hitler, was inclined to straddle fences as he purported to see good and evil commingled on both sides. Germany was at least partially exonerated because the "fiendish menace from Moscow" had misguided her into sanctioning the partitioning of Poland and the subjugation of "an ancient Catholic people." England and France were blameworthy because they lacked the constructive power to encourage the sane Christians of Germany in a fruitful cooperation."[93] Later the Pope authorized the publication of a report by the Roman Catholic primate of Poland on Nazi abuse of the clergy, but again and again it was reiterated that England and France could not be crusaders for a holy cause because they were not Roman Catholic countries.[94]

Hilaire Belloc argued that in a sense every war was a religious war because it compelled a man to make sacrifices for what he worshipped most—in this case "the nation." The Roman Church, he was convinced, stood as the only bulwark that might bring order out of chaos.[95] Meanwhile the Vatican had ceased remonstrating with the Nazi government over its domination of religion and had given *de facto* recognition to the German conquests. Roman Catholics of America were assured: "If the time comes when this war assumes the character of a battle for God against Satan, the Holy Father will recognize that fact and proclaim it." The ambivalence of the Pope at this juncture was excused because he had "insufficient jurisdiction." [96] In 1944, when the plea of Pius XII for a just peace was called appeasement, the retort was that it was only discreet for him to be reticent about Nazi misdeeds from the time of France's collapse until the Allied invasion of Germany.[97]

In the autumn of 1941 the American bishops promulgated a joint declaration entitled "The Crisis in Christianity." Nazism and Communism were simultaneously objurgated as subversive and evil influences contaminating the world. But there was no *en masse* condemnation of the Russian people. Genuine concern was manifested for the Germans suffering under the Hitler regime. The papal exhortation for a just peace was reaffirmed: "Triumph over hate, over mistrust, over the spirit of ruthless selfishness, over the conflict in world economy, over the false principle that might makes right." But full support was pleadged to the war effort.[98]

Roman Catholic moralists drew some fine distinctions in treating problems related to the war. One subject considered was, as the title of the essay put it, "The Supernatural Value of a Soldier's Death." It was asked: "Can a soldier be a martyr?" In righteous crusades which were incontrovertibly just, since they were directed against infidels and helped the propagation of the faith, this would indubitably be the case, was the answer. The conflict then raging could not meet the requirements, however, because its attendant war aims were not clearly defined. Yet it was conceivable that the death of a Roman Catholic soldier might be an act of charity. This promise of divine approval for rendering the supreme sacrifice was based on "the certain doctrine of extra-sacramental justification of a soul by a perfect act of charity." [99]

Dorothy Fremont collected anecdotes and comments from parents and GI's to write a book as a tribute to Roman Catholic chaplains serving in the armed forces. She took pride in recounting their spiritual and military heroism. At the time she wrote, she could boast: "Up to the present time over two thousand Catholic priests have exchanged their clerical garb for the uniform and battle-dress of our American fighting men." [108] Father Duffy, the "legendary" soldier priest and patriot of World War I, was declared to be the symbol of all the Roman Catholic chaplains in World War II. Although the Church opposes war, she refuses to stand idly by while one is in progress, Miss Grant declared. "Always she stands for peace but her Apostles are the comrades of warriors."[181] This is not inconsistent, because the Church must be on hand wherever souls are in danger. "The Apostolate of Soldiers is nothing new. . . . It begins, in fact, with Christ Himself, whose charming consideration for the soldiers of Imperial Rome is so vividly portrayed in the pages of the Gospel." When the Roman officer appealed to the Divine Master for help, "Christ became the first army chaplain in the history of Christianity."[182]

As the Military Vicar of the Armed Forces of the United States, Cardinal Francis J. Spellman of New York City called upon our fighting men to win the military campaigns on land, on sea, and in the air, without neglecting to assume responsibility for leadership in opening up "a second front of prayer." Quotations from famous American Presidents like George Washington and Franklin D. Roosevelt were interwoven, in his book *The Road to Victory,* with references to Thomas Aquinas and declarations from Pope Pius XI setting forth the God-given rights which were worthy of American loyalty. Obedience to the laws of God and the Roman Catholic Church would assure God's favor and the restoration of peace. At the date of writing, four Roman Catholic chaplains had "made the supreme sacrifice for God and country," and others had been wounded and captured. The Church was willing to pay this cost in blood and tears, the prelate said, to obtain peace with justice.[183]

A Roman Catholic chaplain who prefers to remain anonymous has written a book containing recollections of his experiences as a spiritual adviser to American troops in World War II. While reviewing the early war days in Italy, and bemoaning man's folly which ruined so many cities and scarred so many churches, he digresses to remark, "But more ruthless than war, because it parades under the guise of respectability, is the heinousness of birth control and divorce. Soldiers had some means of defense against death from deadly and lethal weapons. Would that the unborn and the children of broken homes were given the same chance against those who would violate the laws of God." He cries "for shame!" at those who "would force such un-Christian teachings on the downtrodden peoples in the world today as a solution to their ills."[184]

Roman Catholics have been in the vanguard among those groups conducting the crusade against world Communism. While the Vatican could arrive at a *modus vivendi* with Mussolini and Hitler, no such compromise has been conceivable with Stalin and his successors. Roman Catholic opinion is unanimous in execrating the Kremlin, whereas it was never fully agreed on how to handle the Fascists and the Nazis.

Thus, Roman Catholics from America serving in the expeditionary forces in Korea could be enjoined to give unequivocal support to a military campaign so remote from our shores, because it was serving to arrest the spread of atheistic Communism. Our action would not be viewed as appeasement or as undertaken in vain if we considered what we would have lost had we not leaped to the defense of South Korea, according to one Roman Catholic opinion. "Those who profess to be so unhappy about our limited achievements in Korea might contrast them with the sight of American cities in rubble and American civilian populations by the tens of thousands burned to a crisp." With this comparison in mind, we could applaud the Korean War "as a repulsion of aggression and strengthening of a free world in the hope of avoiding catastrophe." [185]

C. THE PROTESTANT EPISCOPAL CHURCH

The Anglican Church has historically followed approximately the same war ethics as those of Roman Catholics and Lutherans. The Thirty-nine Articles allow that "it is lawful for Christian men to wear weapons and serve in wars." [186] William Ames set forth the accepted view on war in his *Conscience with the Power and Cases Thereof* (1643). War was always to be regarded as evil, he said, because if one side is in the right the other is bound to be in the wrong. Nevertheless, Christians might participate in good conscience unless they had unmistakable evidence that a war was unjust. The authority of the prince was to be respected. Together with the officers of high rank, he was responsible for determining when it was necessary to go to war. There would invariably be innocent victims. They were to be injured as little as possible.[187]

William Temple, the late Archbishop of Canterbury, once declared: "The duty to fight is a civic duty which, if the cause is good, Christianity accepts and approves." The Archbishop of York was willing to allow that Christians could take part in a "just war" if it was legal and defensive, and if the participants had a reasonable prospect of victory.[188]

Opinion was by no means uniform among Episcopalians, before Pearl Harbor, as to what attitude Americans should adopt toward the European conflagration. But for the most part, there was a leaning toward intervention. The close ties between the Episcopal Church in the United States and the Church of England readily explains why the sympathies of the clergy and membership would favor the Allies. After our involvement there was frequent ecclesiastical endorsement, and much encouragement was given toward a vigorous prosecution of the war to a successful termination.

Seldom did there appear to be much disturbance of conscience over the vicious instruments of warfare that were used. The God-approved justice of our cause was rarely brought into question. After V-J Day *The Living Church* exclaimed: "Victory is ours. . . . Let us indeed rejoice that God, who reigns omnipotent above all battles, has prospered the cause of the United Nations. . . ." No moral indignation was registered over the atomic blasts that reduced Hiroshima and Nagasaki to charred ruins. That the Hague Convention was outmoded and superseded, there was no doubt. That the atomic bomb did not belong to the class of "arms, projectiles, or material of a nature to cause superfluous injury" could not be gainsaid. "But the whole moral atmosphere of the old laws of war has disappeared." Isolationism was no longer possible. The United Nations, it was argued, must function with sufficient force and effective weapons to police the whole world.[189]

Early in 1941 the Episcopal Bishop of Missouri told the members of his diocese that they should back aid for Britain. The times were out of joint and something drastic would have to be done to set them right, he said. Hitler's proposed "wave of the future" would have to be resisted by sending munitions abroad to fortify the island bastion of England.[110]

Militant Dean Beekman, an Episcopal prelate assigned to shepherd a Parisian flock, flayed the Nazis so relentlessly that they compiled a dossier of his sermons and intended to arrest him. But he escaped and returned to America to make "509 speeches in the nation's churches, colleges, and Rotary clubs, pointing out the imminence of German victory if the United States didn't join the Allies." His final tour was even arranged under the auspices of the War Department. After we became embroiled in the conflict, his injunction was: "Don't pray for peace; pray for triumph."[111]

A Baptist minister writing in the *Anglican Review* endeavored to justify Christian military service by applying Schweitzer's "interim theory." The teachings of Jesus must be understood within their eschatological framework, he insisted. Absolute nonresistance

could not be put into practice until the Kingdom was fully established. Besides, Christ did threaten violence, even if He did not
use it. There was a place in the Church for the Christian pacifist,
who kept the ideal situation before us, but also indispensable was
the realist who was ready to cope with the actual danger by resorting to force.[112]

D. CHURCHES IN THE CALVINISTIC TRADITION

In the teachings of John Calvin the omnipotence of the Sovereign God is the dominant principle. The rightfulness or wrong-
ness of any human action must be judged in respect to whether or
not it contributes toward the greater glory of God. The justice or
injustice of a war must be determined by whether or not it is in
conformity with the Will of God. Whenever kings and nations take
up arms to execute God's wrath upon evildoers, they deserve the
loyal support of every Christian. Church and state should be closely
allied in the endeavor to uphold law and order.

Leaning heavily on the Old Testament to mold his theocratic
ideal, Calvin might have been expected to endorse war as a legitimate necessity, and so he did. He wrote: "Princes are armed . . .
also to defend the territories committed to their charge by going to
war against any hostile aggression; and the Holy Spirit, in many
passages of Scripture, declares such wars to be lawful." [113] Going
a step beyond Luther, who sanctioned only defensive war, he
deemed it permissible to send out armies for the infliction of "public
vengeance." [114] He speaks of the enemy as "armed robbers." The
causes underlying war in ancient times were still in existence, he
maintained, so princes could not be blamed for defending their
subjects. War was a device which the state might employ to further
its own mundane interests, "provided only that the aim is just, and
that moral discipline is maintained." [115] The Westminster Confession announced that "It is lawful for Christians . . . to wage war
upon just and necessary grounds."

In the Middle Ages the wars against the Moslems became holy
crusades. Certain elements of the crusade idea reappeared later
among Calvinists. If a war was fought for a worthy ideal, it tended

to become God's war, they maintained. Thus, the Civil War in England came to be regarded as a crusade against the opponents of pure religion. The *Soldier's Pocket Bible* of the Ironsides, written in 1643, quoted against the commandment to "love your enemies" the verses "Dost thou help the wicked and love them that hate the Lord?" (II Chron. 19:2) and "Do not I hate them, O Lord, that hate Thee? . . . I hate them with an unfeigned hatred as they were mine utter enemies" (Psa. 139:21–22). The inference was that the soldier must "love his enemies as they are his enemies and hate them as they are God's enemies." [116] Trevelyan tells how the Puritans made war in the name of their religion: "The Episcopalians were alarmed in 1641 already when they observed how easily their opponents could create *praying regiments* to:

> Decide all controversy by
> Infallible artillery;
> And prove their doctrine orthodox
> By Apostolic blows and knocks.[117]

Orthodox Presbyterians and conservative Reformed churches generally subscribed to Calvin's analysis of war, and were unqualifiedly and uncritically behind the prosecution of World War II.

After the United States became an active participant, Robert Hastings Nichols advised the churches to end all discussion about the possibility of avoiding war. Our people were in this war, he maintained, to overcome tyranny and prevent the spread of totalitarianism. The Church had to learn and teach that this was God's world and that all that transpired was a reflection of His majestic Will. It was the design of God to turn this conflict into good. "The Church . . . surely recognizes that this war is in a good cause. . . . It is a war to preserve our country, its material life and its far more precious spiritual life. It is a war that has been thrust upon us." [118]

In his article "The Christian Stake in Asia," Harry B. Price declared that Japanese militarism was a threat equally as dangerous as Nazi Germany. Our enemies in Asia, he maintained, had used our science and technology for only one purpose—to increase their power so that they could crush the rest of the world and enthrone their emperor as the sublime ruler of all mankind. Their symbol for God was the sword. Christianity had no choice other than to oppose the "New Order" of either Nazism or Nipponism. In his estimation, pacifism was an escape from responsibility. Rather than leading to "purification by suffering," it caused the victims of aggression to be brutalized and embittered. "Better the catastrophe of another war, if freedom can thereby be preserved, than that tyranny should conquer. . . ."[119]

The Reverend Frank B. Everitt expressed concern in the article "The Pastoral Prayer in Wartime." His admonition was that the preacher must beware of propagandizing for either war or peace in public prayer. If the clergyman was a political pacifist, Mr. Everitt maintained, he was entitled to his private convictions, but he did not have a right to drag his feelings into the prayers he used. Prayer during wartime should rather be used to lead people back to God and to "display the uniqueness of our Christian faith." Including a prayer for the enemy would demonstrate the distinctive quality of Christian prayer.[120]

Certain Presbyterians reminded us that a moral force such as non-violence in an aggressive world could be immorally used. To make of pacifism a Trojan Horse movement was no more praiseworthy than for Communists or Nazis to organize subversive cells in a country preliminary to military attack upon us.[121] John Wick Bowman proclaimed, "I believe in the Gospel: I do not believe in war." Most pacifists, as he understood them, belonged to some branch of the Romantic-Humanistic school or otherwise to one of the modern socio-economic groups whose flair was for opposition to the established order. Pacifism would always fail because it ignored the sin in which all human beings were hopelessly enmeshed. Dr. Bowman did not wish popular approval for his stand against war. His appeal was to Christians only, he said. The Gospel of the Divine Sovereignty of God was the sole remedy for the world's ills. War was sin because it interfered with man's opportunity to fulfill his responsibility to love his fellow man.[122]

George Wells Arms offered comparisons between Biblical times and the current scene. What was true of Israel in the days of Jeremiah was still true in our situation today, he argued. The same sins predominated. Many Americans were living in a fool's paradise, boasting about our own self-sufficiency while destruction was threatening and time was running out. Democracy and Protestantism shared in the failure. A true prophet for our day must be one of gloom and pessimism, so it would be impossible for him to enjoy a popular following. We were reaping the bitter fruit of a century of apostasy from God's Word. Scholars in Germany had undermined the Scriptures with their subtle criticisms, and their negative influence had spread to England and America. God's judgment was ripe, and His mode of punishment would be war. He would use one nation to scourge another. Our only hope was in the Second Coming of Christ. Our only shelter of refuge was in the shadow of the Cross.[123]

The influence of the war on contemporary theology was traced by the Reverend Lockhart Amerman. The Calvinistic emphases on original sin and irresistible grace were enjoying a rebirth, he said. With the cataclysm of another world war being added to the crisis of 1921, it was again possible to believe in the total depravity of man. When education had produced Hitlerism and science had invented poison gas, we could not escape the conclusion that our deficiency was in the realm of morals.[124]

Five years after the war had ended, *Presbyterian Life* featured the opposing views of two young veterans in a debate entitled: "Must Christians be Pacifists?" Taking the affirmative position, Mallory Graves recounted how his "secular pacifism" had evaporated when he became convinced that the Nazis might succeed in perpetrating their ideas throughout the world and eradicating all others. He joined the Army, was stationed at Hawaii during the Pearl Harbor attack, and served a total of thirty months overseas. While isolated on a barren island in the Aleutian chain, he recalled, his religious thinking, which had been dormant, was re-awakened. He began to apply Christ's teachings to the problem of war and concluded that it was "the antithesis of all that is Christian." Jesus taught that we should go the way of the Cross, dying rather than killing. It was unthinkable, in his estimation, to imagine Christ dropping a bomb on a heavily populated city and causing death and disease.

Taking the negative stand, Frank H. Heinze argued that "failure to act against evil supports that evil." The law of love did not always imply gentleness and appeasement, he insisted. "War is an immoral expression of an immoral society," but God is capable of converting evil into good.

In commenting on the conflicting sets of arguments, Dr. Ganse Little, President of the Board of Christian Education of The Presbyterian Church, U.S.A., found fault with both and concluded that the issue must finally be decided by the individual Christian conscience seeking the guidance of the Holy Spirit.[125]

The issue of *Presbyterian Life* for February 3, 1951, contained a "special report on Korea." The history of Protestant Christianity in Korea was retold. Pictures of Presbyterian mission work showed people worshipping on sites where churches had been destroyed. Their faith was extolled: "Korean Christians are invincible." The work of Presbyterian missionaries who had stayed in Korea to administer relief to thousands of refugees was described and an appeal was made to relieve the misery of bereaved Korean children. The suffering inflicted by the war was lamented, but the causes of the conflict and the way in which it was being conducted were not considered.[156]

Bible Fundamentalists with an unmistakable Calvinistic strain commingled with certain Anabaptist traits were vociferous in their patriotism at all times. Political and social issues were characteristically intermingled with moral and religious questions in their writings. Opposition to the whole Roosevelt Administration was often vehement. Our pre-Pearl Harbor foreign policy was relentlessly denounced. Some of the popular Fundamentalist leaders were identified with the American First crusade and contended bitterly against the "war-mongers." [157]

The scions of Dwight Moody blamed "unbelief and modernism" for causing the war. Such a gruesome conflagration had arisen, they argued, because "men love darkness rather than light." We had to remember that we had been a "God-forgetting nation." America would have a spiritual responsibility during and after the war. The distressing conditions which prevailed emphasized anew the need for repentance and revival.[128]

A posthumous article by Rev. James M. Gray, explaining "what the Bible teaches about war and the Christian's attitude in the present crisis," was typical of the Fundamentalist stand. The basis for a national declaration of war could be found in the Fifth Commandment and the Genesis edict against the shedding of blood, it was asserted. The government was to be regarded as the executioner of those who had committed murder, whether individuals or whole nations were the culprits. Nations, under God, had magisterial functions to perform in conducting war. In Old Testament wars, Jehovah was often the aggressor against pagan idolaters. Assyria, on the other hand, was the rod of God against Israel punishing her apostasy. If Israel had not taken up the sword against the surrounding peoples, the true religion might have been lost, and she would have defied God. Similarly, if Charles Martel had not fought the Saracens in the eighth century, we might be Mohammedan today. "Few will deny that the victory of Wellington at Waterloo was an act of God." Judged accordingly, the Revolutionary and Civil Wars were essential. And so, by implication, was the present struggle with the Axis Powers. The article went on: Romans 13 demands participation in war. The Old Testament is an authentic guide. The Sermon on the Mount must be understood in the light of Christ's declaration: "I did not come to destroy the Law and the Prophets." What He condemns is limited to retaliation between individuals. Nevertheless, the Christian who has conscientious scruples should be respected.[129]

Apocalyptic references have been scattered throughout the publications of many Fundamentalist groups in recent years. Stalin has been identified with the Anti-Christ, and descriptions of atomic warfare are read into the Book of Revelation. Satan is believed to be increasing in power. Modern wars are sure signs that the world is going to ruin. A catastrophic end to civilization is often predicted. But such pessimism over the world's trek to perdition is matched by a fervent expectancy of divine intervention. For some leaders and sects, this hope is sometimes limited to a confident belief in the imminence of the millenial reign of Christ on earth. Others are sure that religious revivals, like those conducted by Billy Graham, may be expected to ward off the day of judgment and Christianize our culture.[130]

Sometimes, Fundamentalists have said, God exerts His majestic power in overthrowing the wicked designs of men to promote His own Kingdom. The Communists "intended the Korean attack for evil, but God in the mystery of His will has overruled it to ultimate good." Korea was held to be stronger spiritually as a result of the bloody conflict. Before the war there had been only one Christian seminary in the North. The people who migrated South during and following the war had founded three thousand congregations there. The Word of God was spreading. Furthermore, the prisoners-of-war who had once been Communists were rapidly being converted to Christianity after hearing the Gospel in the prisons.[131]

E. THE METHODIST CHURCH

The founders of the Methodist movement in England and America inclined toward the theological position that is historically known as "Arminianism." Most of the controversy in Reformed circles, historically centered around such distinctively Calvinistic doctrines as unconditional election and inadmissibility of grace. Arminians—and their later offspring, the Methodists—veered away from viewing war as a revelation of the eternal and irresistible Will of God. They wanted to allow room for the operation of free choice. Man was more than a mechanically maneuvered object being shifted about on the chessboard of fate according to divine whim. His responsibility in war as well as peace was deemed to be considerable.

Especially pertinent to this discussion was the Arminian disavowal of total depravity. Natural man, the anti-Calvinists said, had the power to obey when the Spirit called. There was in man, since the Fall, the glimmerings of a natural light whereby he retains some knowledge of God, of natural things, and of the difference between good and evil, and discovers some regard for virtue, good order in society, and for maintaining an orderly external deportment. . . .[132] Closely aligned to this belief was the teaching that already in this life the adherent of Christ might arrive at a state of perfection. Limborch, the systematizer of Arminian theology, admitted that "the habit of sinning cannot be exterminated at once," but through persistent effort and gradual development "it is alto-gether extinguished." From this it was only another step to the posi-tion that good works are essential for salvation.[133]

With this theological orientation, it is easy to see why Methodists have always been actively concerned about reform and improve-ment in the political realm. During the heyday of the Social Gospel, Methodism was definitely enamored by the prospects for the estab-lishment of the Kingdom of God on earth. We might expect to find that optimistic hopes for world peace and the betterment of inter-national relations would die slowly where they had been cherished so fondly.

Thus, it is not surprising that spokesmen for the Methodist Church were in the forefront of many pre-World War II peace movements. There was considerable semi-official as well as popular sentiment against militarism during the 'thirties. Many Methodist young men declared their unwillingness to take up arms in another futile crusade to "save the world for democracy." But when the actual war situation came, this feeling rapidly changed. Most Meth-odists were as enthusiastic as other Christians in giving vent to their patriotic emotions. Some members of the Methodist Church pro-tested against the reversal of position that followed Pearl Harbor and remained pacifist, but they were only a small minority.

Perhaps one of the most definitive official Methodist pronounce-ments on the Second World War came in the form of a resolution at the General Conference in Kansas City in 1944. After much debate and committee work, the delegates agreed upon the follow-ing statement:

> Christianity cannot be nationalistic; it must be universal in its outlook and appeal. War makes its appeal to force and hate; Christianity, to reason and love. The influence of a church must, therefore, always be on the side of every effort seeking to remove animosities and prejudices which are contrary to the spirit and teachings of Christ. It does not satisfy the Christian conscience to be told that war is inevitable. It staggers the imagination to contemplate another, with its unspeakable horrors in which modern science will make possible the destruction of whole popu-

lations. The methods of Jesus and the methods of war belong to different worlds. War is a crude and primitive force. It arouses passions which in the beginning may be unselfish and generous, but in the end war betrays those who trust in it. It offers no security that its decisions will be just and righteous. It leaves arrogance in the heart of the victors and resentment in the heart of the vanquished. When the teachings of Jesus are fully accepted, war as a means of settling international disputes will die and, dying, will set the world free from a cruel tyrant. We have looked to international diplomacy to prevent war and it has failed. We have trusted in international law to reduce the horrors and eliminate in a measure the cruelties of war, but war grows only more hideous and destructive. The time is at hand when the Church must rise in its might and demand an international organization which will make another war impossible.[134]

In the autumn of 1944, Georgia Harkness wrote a series of articles entitled "God and the War." The whole problem of evil was posed. The familiar enigma of why the innocent must suffer with the guilty was considered. Readers were reminded that God's Kingdom grew as suffering was banished by self-giving love. "Whatever happens to men, God suffers most."[135]

Dr. Harkness mentioned five ways in which God overcame the hideous evils of war:

God delivers us from evil (1) by imparting courage to those who suffer; (2) by "using any gift that is brought to Him in love for the service of men" (such gifts may be brought by C.O.'s by those on the side of the United Nations, and by persons fighting for the Axis powers); and (3) by "the creation of a community of understanding and love that is world-wide in its scope." The Church holds Christians together in a world fellowship in spite of war (4) by "stirring us to political action to create the conditions of peace"; and (5) by "imparting faith through Christ that the triumph of His Kingdom is sure."[136]

The role of the Church in establishing a lasting peace was a topic of concern at many Methodist conferences and church conventions.[137] Charles A. Ellwood pleaded for an expression of Christian love in the establishment of peace terms according to the Atlantic Charter. From a postwar perspective it can be seen that his admonitions were directed against what proved to be some of the temptations and pitfalls of victory. Specifically, he warned against seeking reprisals, and dividing Germany contrary to the wishes of her people. We "must not give the impression of Anglo-Saxon domination of the world." [138] To prevent economic inequalities, he continued, we should grant access to raw materials on the same terms to all nations.[139] The editor of *The Christian Advocate* commented on the success of the meeting at Dumbarton Oaks. He was exuberant over the agreements reached that committed us to worldwide responsibilities, and the provision made for small nations to participate.[140] Presuming the necessity for an all-out military victory, Norman Huffman inquired "Which Peace Plan?" and sketched some Christian proposals.[141] Bishop G. Bromley Oxnam frankly predicted a third world war by 1975 if "we fail to establish world law and order." [142] He seriously questioned our right to condemn the vengeful reactions of those who had endured the cruelties of war. Dumbarton Oaks, he averred, was a step in the right direction.

Near the end of the conflict there was comment on the recommendation of Congressman Gordon McDonough of California that a Catholic priest, a Protestant minister, and a Jewish rabbi be included in the delegation to a peace conference. It was suggested that church laymen be urged to make a contribution toward a Christian peace. But already a dismal note was introduced because of the trend toward a victors' justice: "There is very little probability that any formal parlays will be held. . . . The Germans and Japanese will be required to accept terms in the formulation of which they will have no part." [143]

The demoralizing effect of the war on the younger generation was seriously deplored. After describing the malnutrition and disease found among the war orphans, Roy L. Smith reminded his readers that "these are the ones who will make the next war!" His plea for food and clothing came under the caption "We Must Make Peace with the Children." [144]

Another striking article, entitled "Bombed Babies," lamented the psychological consequences of bombings on children. Attention was called to a special study entitled *War and Children,* by Anna Freud and Dorothy T. Burlingham.[145] "When Hatred Is Normal" related the story of a fifth-grader who had been sitting under the instruction of a Christian woman in the public school system of a Pennsylvania town. The little girl was mystified by her teacher's attitude: "I don't understand her. She don't hate the Germans. She don't hate the Japs. She don't hate anybody. She's funny, ain't she?"[146]

Sometimes American policy was lauded as indicative of our moral superiority. The heading "Americans Can Be Proud" contrasted the bestiality of the Japanese army in Nanking with the fine treatment accorded one thousand five hundred Japanese prisoners-of-war rounded up by the Federal Government and incarcerated at Missoula, Montana.[147] But some cynics might well have inquired if popular outbursts of ill will against Japanese-Americans and their enforced detention in special camps was likewise praiseworthy. The Hood River, Oregon, post of the American Legion decided to eliminate from the community honor roll the names of fifteen Japanese-Americans serving with the Armed Forces, but later reconsidered and rescinded the order.[148]

The article "Suppose We Win" expressed a premonition: What if, after victory, we found that in fighting the Nazis we had become Nazified ourselves? In bombing German cities, it was intimated, we were no less brutal than the Germans who had bombed London and Coventry. Decrying the militarism of our enemies, we were advocating universal military training for our own youth. Nietzsche was quoted: "When you fight a monster, beware lest you become a monster." The United States was morally responsible for its indulgence of rotten movies, the liquor interests, and racism. "What shall it profit a great nation if it win the war and lose its own soul?"[149] In another issue, the accusation was made that atrocity tales were being fabricated to advance the war loan. This unscrupulous fund-accumulating device was stigmatized as "traffic in the blood and agonies of American boys." The American people, the editors concluded, should be trusted to respond without a base appeal to anger and revenge.[150]

Bishop Wilbur E. Hammaker maintained that the Church should always remain the conscience of the nation. Changes that had been made in the Delaware findings of the Federal Council of Churches' Commission to Study the Bases of a Just and Durable Peace displeased him. He opposed the removal of the explicit assurance that any world organization must be created by all the nations, without the alliances that would naturally evoke counter-alliances, and guaranteeing that the weak would not be dominated by the strong. He was opposed to the protocol "The Six Pillars," issued as part of "The Statement of Political Principles" in the late spring of 1943, which suggested that the United Nations continue their collaboration after the war was over, and include the neutral and enemy nations in their organization eventually. This trend was flouted as a "compromise." [151]

The Protestant pulpit was congratulated, in *The Christian Advocate*, for exercising more restraint in the Second World War than in the First. Although the "Salesmen of Hate" were not as blatant this time as last, the magazine said, we might live to rue "the unreasoning virulence with which large numbers of Americans hate everything Japanese." [152] Chaplain Howell G. Guin discovered that every nation looked upon itself as a peace-loving people, forced against its will to wage war. Japan, Italy, and Germany had all made protests of innocence. Their soldiers were persuaded in their own minds that they were fighting in a just cause. German prisoners asked: "Why do you Americans fight us?" Their belt-buckles were stamped with the motto: *Gott mit uns*. Wars would not cease, Chaplain Guin warned, when those who had been declared guilty were punished by the victors.[153]

Several published prayers for victory were characterized by their humility, their acknowledgment of our own guilt, and their concern for the enemy. The Reverend W. Arthur Faus prayed:

> Infinite Father, in deep penitence we confess that not once but many times we have strayed far from Thee in our attitudes and conduct. . . . We commend to Thy care the

millions of young men of all nationalities who are plunged into the holocaust of war. Whatever their race or creed or nation, they are Thy children. Keep them spiritually safe even when they cannot all be kept physically safe. Grant, O God, that in some way this scourge of war may soon be brought to an end and the Christ spirit of aggressive love, universal justice, and magnanimous forgiveness may increasingly dominate the nations and peoples of the world. Amen.[154]

A verse prayer for victory read:

> From vain display and pride of power,
> From every boastful word,
> From all decisions that mercy shun,
> Deliver us, Good Lord.
>
> O God, Whose aid our fathers sought,
> In crises of the past,
> Help us a righteous peace to gain,
> And stablish it at last.
>
> We humble crave Thy pardon, Lord.
> Our nation went astray.
> We failed as sentries of the Peace,
> And now its foes we slay.
>
> The aims and language that they shout
> We must not imitate,
> But strive to win a better world,
> Where love can blot out hate.
>
> We seek a democratic peace,
> That shall forever guard
> The common man, in every land.
> So grant us victory, Lord.[155]

A defense against accusations of American imperialism was combined with an expression of confidence in the power of Christ's religion to transform men and abolish war, in *Motive*, the Methodist student magazine:

Paul called himself a slave of Christ, but it was slavery of love, not of force; it meant freedom of Spirit. For this freedom Paul fought. . . . We believe that love and mutual goodness of all peoples are mightier than totalitarian slavery and military weapons; we believe that the most certain means of abolishing war is found in the spirit of the Cross. The U. S. is for freedom—defend it![156]

F. Pacifist Christians

Even before the sixteenth century, dissenting religious groups such as the Waldenses and the Moravian Brethren protested against Christian collaboration in armed conflicts. Under Menno Simons and Anabaptist leadership, during the Reformation period, a non-resistance position developed that has influenced pacifists down to the present day. The Mennonite demand for absolute separation from the world and emphasis on the external purity of the Church has included abstinence from war-making. Mennonites have usually remained aloof from all political and economic affairs which were identified with the sinfulness of the world. They render obedience to the "government of the world" only in those things "which do not militate against the Law, will, and commandments of God."[157] Menno Simons declared:

The regenerated do not go to war nor fight. They are the children of peace who have beaten their swords into plowshares and their spears into pruning hooks and know of no war. . . . All who accept our doctrine in its power, will by God's grace not have any ill will to any one upon earth, and not against their most bitter enemies, much less wrong and harm them by deeds and actions.[158]

Jakob Hutter wrote to the Governor of Moravia in the same vein in 1535:

Ere we would knowingly do injustice to anybody for a penny's worth, we would rather suffer to be deprived of a hundred florins, and to be wronged. And ere we would strike our worst enemy with our hand, let alone with the pike, sword, or halberd, as the world does, we would rather die and have our lives taken from us.[159]

A Hutterite ordinance issued in Slovakia in 1633 pleaded: "We ask for the sake of Christ that you would desist from rioting, beating, pushing around, scrambling for work, and like acts of violence. They all are nothing but sin." [160]

The Anabaptists refused to recognize any references to the Old Testament which could not be harmonized with the New. In a debate at Frankenthal the Swiss Brethren affirmed: "We believe that the New Testament surpasses the Old. So much of the Old Testament as is not irreconcilable with the doctrine of Christ, we accept. . . ." [161]

Mennonites in America have a Peace Problems Committee which was enlarged in 1925 and which has attempted to carry on a threefold program calling for: "(1) A plan of education on non-resistance within the church, (2) for keeping in touch with government officials, and (3) for witnessing to the nonresistant faith among other groups." [162]

During the Second World War an argument arose among Mennonites as to whether it would be proper for them to petition the government to pass laws according favorable treatment to their members who desisted from military service. The Peace Problems Committee took the initiative in appearing before government committees and lawmakers to testify in behalf of the Mennonite position. But this church did not take an extreme position opposing registration and conscription. It was ready to grant that the government could not be expected to function without the use of penalties and the power of coercion.

It is surprising to learn, however, that in a church which opposes war in principle almost forty per cent of the men drafted went into the Army. Many members worked in armament factories. Social pressures and economic advantages have been suggested as the primary reasons why some of the Mennonite laity acted contrary to the traditional position of their denomination.

Opposition arose, within and without the church, to the plan of using members of the church as camp directors to enforce Selective Service regulations upon the men under their control. A statistical evaluation of the experiences of the young men serving in Civilian Public Service camps has seemed to indicate that their religious

loyalties were reinforced there. It is felt that the contacts effected
with other divisions of Mennonites and other pacifist denominations
at the C.P.S. camps were highly valuable. The scattering of the
C.O.'s into work camps at different geographical locations is said
to have had the beneficial effect of enlarging the vision of the
church.

To show that it was unwilling to help directly in the financing of
the war, the church presented a plan by which members could buy
"civilian bonds" instead of war bonds. Some members thought that
this was only a subterfuge which still released money for the war
effort, however, so they preferred to donate money for the relief of
war victims.[163]

The Church of the Brethren, originating in Germany early in
the eighteenth century, adopted views similar to those upheld by
the Mennonites. The original Brethren community practiced nonresistance. The early Brethren, both in Germany and in America,
did not participate in war. In his book *The History of Pennsylvania*, published in 1798, Robert Proud commented on this segment
of the population: "They also hold it not becoming a follower of
Jesus Christ to bear arms or fight; because, say they, their true
Master has forbid His disciples to resist evil." [164] In the Petition of
the Mennonites and Brethren to the House of Representatives of
Pennsylvania, offered on November 7, 1775, the following statement was made: ". . . we have dedicated ourselves to serve all
men in everything that can be helpful to the preservation of Men's
lives, but we find no Freedom in giving, or doing, or assisting in
anything by which Men's lives are destroyed or hurt." [165]

Strong testimonies for peace were maintained in annual conference pronouncements of the Brethren. A year and a half after the
Second World War started, one such conference declared "that in
the midst of the present tragic war the church's historic conviction
that violence in the relations of men is contrary to the spirit of
Christ must be reaffirmed." [166] During the height of the war's fury,
a year later, the Brethren emphatically reaffirmed their peace principles, fully aware of the way in which many of their members
were compromising with the war system.[167] A survey had indicated
that about 8.5 per cent of the Brethren men drafted had gone

directly into the armed services, about 11 per cent had taken non-combatant service, and 8.5 per cent were in Civilian Public Service camps.

Why this disparity between profession and performance? According to the replies received from questionnaires sent to local churches, the young men who had gone into the Army listed a number of reasons why they had done so: duty to country, social pressure, the economic problem, inadequate peace teaching, the feeling that the war was forced upon them, indifference to the doctrines of the church, and lack of sympathy with the C.O. position. And "there were more strong militarists among the Brethren in World War II than in World War I, and they were more vocal." [168] Surveys showed that requiring a pledge from members not to go to war as a covenant of church membership was dropped by 62 per cent of the churches. However, the great majority of church leaders continued to support the peace teachings of the Brethren throughout the war. They were concerned, after the war, that their testimony for peace would be weakened because a large number of young men had been vitally affected by constant exposure to war propaganda, and a large number of older adults had gained economically from working in defense industries.

Quakers, too, have been a part of the pacifist front. For the warlike character of Cromwell's Puritanism they substituted a humanitarian outlook. They objected to war, not only as a violation of love, but as a carnal pursuit which refused to await the unity produced by the Inner Light. Since they had faith in the Light that lights every man, they did not isolate themselves from the common life even in the political sphere, but eagerly participated in affairs of government up to the point of participation in war. [169] William Penn tried to govern Pennsylvania according to Quaker ideals, with "no need of coercive or compulsive means." But after seventy-five years the "holy experiment" failed because funds were being appropriated for military operations and political problems had fostered a bitter struggle among contending groups. [170]

Quakers have long been admired for their sacrificial willingness to contribute for the physical relief of war-torn areas. Already, after the First World War, they issued a manifesto declaring "that peace can only be attained by refusing to take any part in war, for the simple and wholly sufficient reason that war by its whole nature is in opposition to the message and spirit of the life and death of Jesus Christ. . . . The idea of peace . . . demands the most determined repudiation of war, unambiguously and without compromise. . . .[171]

Liberal theology has often been sympathetic toward Christian Pacifism. Noah Worcester, a New England minister who founded the Massachusetts Peace Society in 1815, believed that the scourge of war could be wiped out completely within a hundred years through a program of education for peace.[172] William Ellery Channing, his Unitarian contemporary, wanted to end war through the influence of progressive knowledge and refinement. The Social Gospel advocates of the early twentieth century expected to attain a peaceful world by improving man's social environment.

In 1925 the Episcopal General Convention declared that "the nations of the world must adopt a peace system . . . built on the conviction that war is unchristian in principle and suicidal in practice." [173] In 1929 the Presbyterian General Assembly renounced "war as an instrument of national policy." [174] In 1933 the Federal Council of Churches urged the continuation of negotiations for world disarmament and the abolition of such "aggressive weapons" as the bombing plane.[175] According to a *World Tomorrow* survey, a 62-per-cent majority of the Protestant ministry was inclined toward pacifism in 1934.[176]

Many such believers in nonviolence fell from the ranks when the sentiment for peace diminished, especially after the attack on Pearl Harbor continued to condemn war as inherently wrong. They wanted to repudiate war as an instrument of national policy. A number of them were persuaded that they could give the most effective witness by forming an organization, the Fellowship of Reconciliation. Its monthly magazine, published during the war years, provided an excellent summary of the pacifist interpretation of events.

Readers of American news releases and sensational magazine reports were horrified by revelations of Nazi and Japanese brutality. Pacifist writers, however, asseverated that war itself was the real atrocity, which evoked the worst in human nature. R. Alfred Hassler suggested that atrocity stories were generalized from occasional incidents and were exaggerated for propaganda purposes. As far as he was concerned, the Anglo-American naval blockade of Europe would likewise have to be classified as an atrocity.[177] A letter to the *New York Times* indicated that Red Cross delegates were allowed to visit most Japanese prison camps, and that they "found no atrocities, but reasonably good conditions, including hot baths weekly and medical attention."[178] From Pearl Harbor Day to January 7, 1944, United States forces had taken only 377 Japanese prisoners.[179] Pacifist critics wondered: Were the Japanese really such unrelenting fighters that they resisted capture, or were Americans indulging in vicious and unrestricted slaughter?

The advocates of reconciliation regretted that Americans were blinded by hatred from seeing the Japanese viewpoint. To the Orientals, America and Britain were the symbols of oppression and imperialism. They had suffered indignity and humiliation at Western hands and resented the Occidental assumption of superiority. At Versailles the English-speaking nations had refused to insert a declaration of racial equality in the peace treaty.[180] We had refused any modification of the 5–5–3 naval ratio. So December 7, 1941, was the launching of a holy crusade, for millions of Japanese. Were we not reaping the bitter harvest of growing ill will derived from the evil seeds that had been planted ever since Commodore Perry had first forced his entrance into Tokyo Bay?

In a series of articles the Englishwoman Vera Britain contested the prudence as well as the morality of our mass bombings. She challenged the validity of the familiar argument that it would shorten the war. Should we not be chagrined, she asked, when reminded that the same excuse was used by the Germans in World War I for their *Schrecklichkeit* (submarine warfare), and for their destructive bombing in World War II of Warsaw, Rotterdam, Belgrade, London, and Coventry? The fact was, more might be killed in one such concentrated raid than would die in weeks of ordinary fighting. Besides, most of the victims of bombings were helpless civilians, including women and children. Mass bombing was purported to induce revolt and break morale. Did it accomplish this aim, Miss Britain asked, or did it, rather, increase the will to resist?[181]

Vera Britain was convinced that the argument based on revenge was equally fallacious. The popular feeling was that the Germans had started the war, and so deserved no sympathy. But George Bernard Shaw was cynical about Allied pretenses to righteousness: "The blitzing of the cities has carried war this time to such a climax of infernal atrocity that all recriminations on that score are ridiculous. The Germans will have as big a bill of atrocities against us as we against them if we take them into an impartial international court." [182] Those who clamored for pitiless vengeance forgot that some of the tactical devices and machines of destruction used against Germany were not known at the time of the raids against England. The pacifist verdict was that "retaliation in kind and worse means the reduction of ourselves to the level of our opponents, whose perverted values have persuaded us to fight." [183]

George L. Paine, in his article "Thoughts on the Treatment of Germany," questioned the propriety of using the terms "Nazi" and "German" as equivalents. With more than a million Germans in concentration camps, it appeared that there must have been more than token resistance to Hitler's regime. The underground movement in Germany was a constant "thorn in the flesh" to the party chieftains. Harsh treatment of Germans would be a stupid policy for us to pursue. It would only provoke another war, unless we were malevolent enough to require complete dismemberment of the German nation, to castrate all German men, or to exterminate the German people. Germany could best be prevented from seeking new conquests by granting her "ready access to the markets of the world both for buying and selling" and by aiding her "in attaining economic prosperity." Mr. Paine reminded his readers that forgiveness was a basic ingredient of the Christian faith. The late Archbishop of Canterbury had stated after the outbreak of war: "We must look forward to the renewed friendship with the German people." [184]

Nels F. S. Ferre contended that the Church should always stand for reconciliation. During the intervals of peace "the Church must labor to effect such conditions as will make war unnecessary." By its message and its position the Church must pass judgment upon the outcroppings of evil in the world. In witnessing to the "purpose of God in Christ Jesus" it would have an ameliorating influence. The Church dared not become enveloped in the fervor of extreme nationalism. It must act as a mediator, "pointing out continually the faults and evils on both sides as well as the good causes on both sides. . . ." Healing the wounds and bitterness of war was "another concrete task of the Church." [185]

The V-E Day statement issued by the National Executive Committee of the Fellowship of Reconciliation pleaded for clemency and amnesty:

> In the name of common sense and humanity we . . . urge the President to state publicly specific terms of settlement with Japan which will provide a worthy place for the Japanese and all other Oriental peoples in an orderly, democratic world society and on this basis to call for the immediate cessation of hostilities in the Orient.[186]

Pacifists repeatedly registered their disapproval of our postwar treatment of the enemy. The division of Germany was denounced as cruel folly. Glenn D. Everett charged that "starvation is our policy." He showed how enforced boundary changes ordered by the Big Three were causing millions to go hungry. "The diet of Germany has been officially set at 1,550 calories a day, 450 calories below the minimum subsistence level of 2,000 calories set for the rest of Europe, and less than half of the average American diet of 3,300 calories." [187]

Dr. Channing Leem of Korea, formerly Professor of Political Science at the Pennsylvania College for Women, would have eliminated the Korean War and guaranteed victory for the United Nations without battle by first assuring the Koreans that their needs would be satisfied, and secondly by distributing everywhere the goods which the poverty-stricken inhabitants lacked. "Let the United Nations try this for one month," he wrote, "and fighting will cease." He contended that "the acute poverty of the Korean people did much to invite the crisis . . ." and "what the Koreans want is independence and economic livelihood." [188]

The refusal of the pacifist to bear arms has often been condemned as cowardly or unrealistic. But most Christian pacifists could rightfully deny this harsh judgment. Those who disagree with the pacifist stand tend to overlook the eloquent witness for peaceful living in the community and reconciliation among the nations which is rendered by these groups during wartime, when hatred and jingoism have blinded the vision of so many leaders within the churches.

But there are difficult questions facing the person who takes this position. He must ask himself: "How can I consistently be a pacifist when my country is engaged in total war? Does not civilian service also involve a Christian in the support of a war economy?" Unless the pacifist wants to isolate himself completely from society and make no contribution whatever to anything, the best he can say is that he is not directly involved in the killing. But is such an argument reasonable? Does it not represent an unsound view of the world, of history, and of human nature in a basic assumption that violence and conflict can be eliminated? Many modern pacifists share with liberal Christians a naïve faith in social progress through education. Then, too, the inquiry may be made: Is perpetual peace on earth a real possibility, or can we only strive for a relative and transitory peace? Is it never possible that the use of force may result in at least the lesser of two evils?

Pacifism must cope with the objections that it is utopian and not relative to the concrete historical situations which arise, and that military necessity (the achievement of victory) may require that a Christian attack the enemy.

4

~~~~~~~~~~~~~~~~~~~~~~~~~~~~~~~~~~~~~

The Christian Conscience on Trial,
1939-19__?

Regarding the role of American churches in World War II and the Korean War, it should be stated that, on the whole, they displayed more self-restraint and equanimity than they did during the First World War. The pulpit was rarely used to issue the call to arms or to fan the embers of hatred. Loyalty to flag and country was stressed, but the extreme emotional outbursts that discredited the clergy in 1917–1918 were generally avoided. None the less, the churches did tend to follow rather than guide public opinion. When the preservation of neutrality was a popular theme, many preachers supported it with sermons and public addresses. When the tide of conflict swept in, most of the churchmen maintained a discreet silence or held up the war banner. A small minority continued to speak out against policies with which they disagreed. The courageous few protested against extreme abuses.

Prior to our actual embroilment in World War II, many members of The Lutheran Church—Missouri Synod were sympathetic toward the America First movement. During the 'thirties, when the real aims of the Nazis were little understood, some Lutherans frankly admired the achievements of the Hitler regime. But after December 1941 there were few who did not join in the clamor for complete victory over the dastardly foe.

This branch of American Lutheranism was distinguished for its unequivocal support of the war effort and its almost unqualified endorsement of every government policy. On the part of the executive leadership, and most of the clergy, there seemed to be an underlying dread that the patriotism of the church might be suspect because of the German background of its constituency. The unpleasant experiences of the First World War, when services in German were rudely interrupted, and when indignities were heaped upon some of the pastors by zealous chauvinists, undoubtedly influenced the "official" attitude assumed from 1941 to 1945. One will search the publications of this church in vain for any critical observations on governmental decisions. In some instances its spokesmen appear almost to have "leaned over backwards" to assure Washington that Missouri Lutherans were dependable soldiers and loyal citizens. If any member of the church expressed misgivings about fighting, he was reminded of the obedience to government required by Romans 13, and perhaps "comforted" with a few quotations from Luther to show "that soldiers too can be saved."

The official attitude of the United Lutheran Church was quite similar, but allowed for a greater latitude of opinion. Individual pastors were vigorous in their dissent. A few sensed that it might be well to reconsider the application of Luther's teachings and the Confessions to participation in modern war. Conscientious objectors were not encouraged in their stand, but they were treated with sympathetic appreciation for their scruples.

The position of the Roman Catholic Church might best be characterized as opportunistic. With papal adherents in both camps, this church was cautious in its declarations. Its policy wavered back and forth, according to the turn of events. As long as ecclesiastical interests were not molested, there was no official Roman Catholic opposition to Hitler and Mussolini. American priests were in the forefront of the "stay-out-of-war" crusade, but rallied to the colors after we became involved. Some Roman Catholic editors tried to call a halt in the march down the road toward war before Pearl Harbor, and resumed their editorial jibes at the Administration as soon as peace was secured.

Reading the wartime issues of *The Christian Advocate* will convey certain general impressions to the reader. In spite of the tragic upheaval through which the world was passing, the editors preserved a rather optimistic outlook for the future. Permanent peace was more than an elusive and unattainable mirage, they maintained. It was a distinct possibility, if only Christian principles were invoked. They did not entirely abandon the "liberal" view of human nature. There were still considered to be some innate good qualities in man which could be developed and utilized in the formation of a more stable and harmonious society. The heritage of Arminian theology, with its denial of man's utter depravity, was still in evidence in these articles. A residue of moral zeal from the era of the Social Gospel survived even during World War II. Thus, Methodists were reliable propagandists in backing the United Nations. Writers waxed enthusiastic in their postwar visions of "one world." No one seemed to feel compelled to adopt an eschatological outlook that would suggest the deterioration of our civilization and the approach of Doomsday.

One glaring inconsistency can be detected in these articles. Fascism and Nazism were invariably singled out for abusive denunciation, while the menace of atheistic Communism was completely ignored. Along with most other denominations, Methodists fell into line as regards the Moscow-Washington alliance and were, for the most part, undisturbed by the incongruity involved. Religious journalists in general were hoodwinked by the outward allegiance which American Communists offered our government as long as it served their own purposes. The rude awakening did not come until after the Yalta and Potsdam agreements and the rupture in East-West relations.

In all fairness, however, it should be mentioned that in other respects Methodist writers were not "blind followers of the blind." Their editorials were discerning, and at times provocative. But after Pearl Harbor there was usually an unquestioning acceptance of the righteousness of our arms, and an understandable reluctance to censure political and military decisions propounded in pursuit of victory. One searches Methodist writings in vain for bristling moral indignation over the atomic massacre at Hiroshima or the vengeful Morgenthau plan to reduce Germany to an agricultural state.

During the controversy over whether or not the United States should back the government of Chiang Kai-Shek, some observers claim that Methodists displayed a certain pro-Chiang bias. The

Christian sympathies of the Generalissimo and the Methodist persuasion of his wife might have been expected to merit favorable reactions from the American Church. While State Department officials disparaged the Generalissimo's integrity and administrative sagacity, and rumors hinted at marital infidelity on his part, loyal Methodists answered such charges promptly and vehemently. They termed the insinuations malicious and unfounded.

Pacifists were found in most of the major Protestant denominations, in addition to the sects in which pacifism is an avowed tenet of faith. Not all pacifists were of an identical mind. Some refused to collaborate in any way with the promotion of the war. Others agreed to go to work camps and accept non-combatant duty with the armed forces or other federal agencies.

Although the author does not find the pacifists' position tenable in its entirety, he does have the conviction that we can learn from the useful witness which they provided in their utter rejection of war. Their emphasis on reconciliation, during the years when other professed Christians were urging hatred and vengeance, seemed as refreshing as a cool breeze during a scorching hot day. While the larger and long-established denominations were compliant, if not servile, in their observance of government directives, the convinced pacifists withstood the pressure of mass persuasion and retained their distinctive principles. While other Christians were cowed into silence, they protested against unnecessary and revolting brutalities. When peace was declared, they were among the first to offer relief supplies to war-stricken areas without discrimination against the former enemy.

In view of the maze of evidence to be weighed, the individual Christian may find himself in a quandary when called upon to voice his convictions concerning the Second World War. The conflicting judgments passed by churchmen only add to the layman's bewilderment. What valid and demonstrable conclusions can we reach? Perhaps in the nature of the case we cannot avoid a certain degree of subjectivity, and should hasten to admit that our evaluations are not final and absolute. Only eleven years have elapsed since the cessation of hostilities, and we cannot yet focus everything that transpired into its proper historical perspective. Nor is more than a particle of the testimony needed to ascertain the motives of states-men and governments in the hands of competent historians.

But this does not imply, as has so frequently been asserted in the Lutheran Church, that since we knew so little about what was taking place, we could not be held accountable. Ignorance is a lame excuse for an uncritical submission to the status quo or a gullible conformity with prevailing opinion. Christians, and particularly the leaders of the Church, if they had used the sources of information available, and if they had seriously attempted to define the issues at stake, could have been a much more potent force in restraining evil and promoting peace. It is the hope of the writer that a critical review of the Church's role in World War II and the Korean War may serve as a deterrent against a repetition of the same failings in the current Cold War crisis and in any future wartime situations.

In conducting this analysis, it will be helpful if we first raise the basic question: Is war, from the Christian standpoint, ever justi-fied? Then it may be instructive and clarifying if, in retrospect, we inquire: Was the Second World War justified? Finally, we must continue our criticism of the American churches and point up their shortcomings in interpreting the God-intended significance of the war to their members, and their inefficacy in sharpening the con-science of our people and calling the nation to repentance.

Most Christians would readily agree that war is deplorable. They have usually concurred with the verdict of disillusioned mili-tarists like Napoleon, who is supposed to have said: "The more I study the history of the world, the more I am convinced of the inability of brute force to create anything durable." Or they assent to the peremptory affirmation of General Moltke: "The most vic-torious war is a misfortune, not only for the conquered, but for the conquerors as well." Sometimes the observation of Sir Walter Scott is echoed: "War is the only game in which both sides lose."

Most Protestant Christians would be quick to maintain that war is not a rightful means for propagating the Gospel. The religious wars of the past have been decried as perversions of the teachings of Christ, who said that His Kingdom was not of this world, and who rebuked His disciples when, in their anger, they wanted to destroy an unfriendly Samaritan village by fire. St. Paul's descrip-

tion of warfare is often called to mind: "For though we live in the
world we are not carrying on a worldly war, for the weapons of
our warfare are not worldly but have divine power to destroy
strongholds" (II Cor. 1:3–5). The Roman Catholic Church is frequently berated for having made conversions by the sword and
for relying upon force to uphold its favored position in areas like
Spain and Latin America.

In principle, many members of the American clergy will insist
that they are opposed to war. They recognize that war is caused
by insolence, greed, and strife. It will be conceded by everyone
that some wars have been downright wicked and stupid, no matter
from whose side we examine them. When a war actually breaks
out, however, seldom have more than a few courageous voices ever
been raised in opposition. The fact is that the majority of clerics
have always rationalized their compliance with the decisions of
temporal authority.

How, in such circumstances, is war justified? The usual argument
follows the line of reasoning that, although war may be evil, surrender to a wanton conqueror would be even worse. The government
that exists is established by God, it continues, and has the right to
execute an evildoer. At times this "evildoer" may be a whole nation
that is waging war against your nation. Unless you are in possession
of unmistakable evidence to prove that your government is following
the wrong course, you are duty bound as a Christian citizen to rise
to arms as commanded.

Under what circumstances *can* war be considered justifiable?
The usual Lutheran response includes the following cases:

1. When war is necessary to preserve the life of the government, threatened by internal insurrection.
2. When the territory of the nation is invaded or threatened with invasion; in defence of honor.
3. When war is the only way in which a nation can be
   true to its treaty obligations, the said obligations themselves being such as a righteous government may incur.
4. When war is the only way, in a given situation, to protect the people entrusted for protection to the government, without yielding to open wickedness.

5. When the highest interest of mankind is at stake, and a country can help, even if not directly threatened.[1]

The present writer is of the opinion that the traditional Lutheran concept of the "just war," as expressed here, and as developed earlier by men like Augustine, Luther, and Gerhard, needs to be reconsidered and modified in recognition of our changed world, the complicated problems arising from the deadly devices employed in modern warfare, and the interdependence and close proximity of the inhabitants of "one world." For instance, it must be realistically decided whether or not in the future any war could conceivably achieve any of the results once claimed for a "just war." Whole cities can now be reduced to ruins and entire populations can be exterminated. The cost of waging war is prohibitive. The economy of the "victor" nations after World War II was hopelessly upset, and a semblance of stability could be maintained only with American aid.

Even if we were, for the sake of further discussion, to assume the validity of the "just war" concept, could we fit our struggle against Germany and Japan into that category? Was this a just war in the traditional sense, or by any acceptable definition of the term?

Most American ministers were assured of the justice of our cause by the Japanese attack on Pearl Harbor, which was pictured to them as an act of unwarranted aggression. Whereas many had contended vigorously against our entrance into war before December 7, 1941, they changed their minds immediately when our Hawaiian outpost was endangered. Presto! We were involved in a war of self-defense, and the "great debate" between interventionists and isolationists was abruptly ended.

But the case is not quite that simple. Those who are familiar with the history of Japanese-American relations still have their doubts. They know that American interests in the Orient had often been selfish and imperialistic. They know all too well of the blunders in our Far Eastern policy that were at least partially responsible for the ascendancy of a fanatical militarist leadership in Japan. Since the war some noted American historians have demonstrated that the Japanese attack was not the unexpected surprise that we had been induced to believe it was, and that it cannot be fairly

described as "unprovoked aggression." We had gradually maneuvered Japan into a position in which she had no choice but to "lose
face" or fight.[2]

Regardless of the sincerity of the leaders involved, and without
impugning motives, the impartial observer cannot help but conclude that the Roosevelt Administration was guilty of duplicity
during the pre-war years and afterwards.[3] While the American
people were led to believe that their government was doing everything possible to avoid war, the President and the State Department were actually committed to an Allied victory over Germany.
They tried by every means "short of war" to insure that victory,
but when these tactics failed, they deemed our entrance into the
war inevitable—all the while permitting the people to believe that
we would not interfere in Europe or Asia.

Former Congresswoman Clare Boothe Luce charged Roosevelt
with having lied us into war. Professor Thomas A. Bailey, a Roosevelt sympathizer, has admitted that deception was used, but attempts to justify it in this way:

> Franklin Roosevelt repeatedly deceived the American peo-
> ple during the period before Pearl Harbor. . . . He was
> like the physician who must tell the patient lies for the
> patient's own good. . . . The country was overwhelmingly
> noninterventionist to the very day of Pearl Harbor, and
> an overt attempt to lead the people into war would have
> resulted in certain failure and an almost certain ousting of
> Roosevelt in 1940, with a complete defeat of his ultimate
> aims. . . . A President who cannot entrust the people with
> the truth betrays a certain lack of faith in the basic tenets
> of democracy. But because the masses are notoriously
> shortsighted and generally cannot see danger until it is at
> their throats, our statesmen are forced to deceive them
> into an awareness of their own long-run interests. This is
> clearly what Roosevelt had to do, and who shall say that
> posterity will not thank him for it?[4]

The author recalls that the same line of argumentation was used in
classes which he attended in 1945 and 1946 at Washington University in St. Louis.

In connection with the "just war" idea, the disturbing question might be raised: Who took the aggressive action that first caused the drift of our nation toward war? Hitler scrupulously avoided any incident that would stir up American war fever as the sinking of the *Lusitania* had done during the First World War. Yet we were pushed step by step into an undeclared war in the Atlantic, months before Pearl Harbor. Almost at the outset the original Neutrality Law was amended to permit "cash and carry" transactions, which in actuality meant that the Allies were given access to war materials which they could purchase in America, while it was impossible for their enemies to take advantage of the same provision. In April 1940 the Committee to Defend America by Aiding the Allies was launched. A bellicose minority began to clamor for intervention. Several admirals advocated a declaration of war.[5] In April 1941 the Fight for Freedom campaign was organized, with the Episcopal Bishop Henry N. Hobson as chairman. Its propaganda posters, such as the one showing a uniformed Nazi bludgeoning an American and shouting, "Shut up, Yank! Learn to speak Nazi!", were designed to scare the country into war.

The America First Committee, which arranged mass demonstrations to protest the drift toward war, was assailed as a "Nazi transmission belt." [6] By subtle innuendo its leaders were associated with the notorious American Destiny Party of Joseph McWilliams and the Silver Shirts of William Dudley Pelley.[7] Cunningly devised campaigns vilified patriots like Senator Wheeler and Colonel Lindberg as pro-Fascist and anti-Semitic.[8]

It would be ridiculous to contend that the United States was an innocent bystander preserving a genuine neutrality in the conflict between the Axis and Allied powers from September 1939 to December 1941. Winston Churchill has quoted Harry Hopkins as having already given him a categorical pledge of all-out American aid in January 1941.[9] Almost unlimited subsidies of munitions and supplies were conveyed to European ports after the passage of the Lend-Lease Act in March of the same year. Meanwhile, important American and British military-staff talks were being conducted in Washington in an atmosphere of extreme secrecy. The principal conclusions reached at these meetings were phrased in a way that took eventual American participation in the war for granted.[10] Another milestone toward war was the decision to use American naval forces to guarantee the safe delivery of cargoes intended for Britain. United States warships and planes were used to search for German raiders and submarines, and broadcast their positions to the Royal Navy. The next move was a "shoot-at-sight" campaign against Axis submarines, invoked in September. By November the President had succeeded by a narrow margin in gaining Congressional approval for the arming of American merchant ships that were to be kept into war zones. Other measures taken by the Administration during 1941 to bring about the downfall of Germany included the sending of American laborers to build a naval base in Northern Ireland, the blocking of German credits in the United States, and the occupation of Iceland by American troops. What this added up to was a deliberate movement toward intervention on the part of the executive branch of our government. The underlying motives of our leaders in promoting this course of action cannot easily be ascertained. The most charitable interpretation is that they were fully persuaded that the Berlin-Tokyo alliance was a threatening menace that had to be extirpated at any cost. The historical facts, however, are indisputable. There can be no doubt regarding the repeated and persistent violations of our professed neutrality. There was an obviously wide gap between our pretensions and our actual deeds.

A studied appraisal of our relations with Japan will show that in the Pacific, too, our justification of the war was not in full accord with the underlying facts. Throughout the Sino-Japanese conflict our sympathies had lain with Chiang Kai-Shek. China had been granted a number of loans and declared eligible for lend-lease aid. In July 1941 the President froze all Japanese assets in this country. This action amounted to an economic blockade of Japan, which drove her to take desperate counter-measures. It certainly weakened the position of the Japanese moderates, who were trying to prevent the militaristic extremists from seizing control. Rather than continue truce negotiations, in the autumn of that year, Secretary of State Hull handed the Japanese envoys a set of ten proposals that amounted to a demand for unconditional surrender. If Japan had submitted to them, it would have meant complete withdrawal of her forces from China and Indo-China. An Army board which later investigated the Pearl Harbor attack described Hull's communication as "the document that touched the button that started the war." [11]

Journalists and historians will probably be writing interpretations of the infamous event of December 7, 1941, for many years to come. The controversy has raged long and furiously as to where the responsibility for the debacle lies. The most gracious judgment will have to assume that it was the result of a lack of foresight and that we were simply caught "off guard." More severe is the conclusion reached by a number of recognized historians who adduce abundant data to argue that Pearl Harbor was the result of a behind-the-scenes attempt to maneuver the Japanese into firing the first shot. [12]

Regardless of how we interpret the evidence, this much is incontrovertible: Our entrance into the war was not occasioned by a direct act of premeditated, uninstigated aggression on the part of the enemy, and ecclesiastical approval of Christian participation could scarcely be grounded on such contention.

Nor is it possible to formulate a convincing case for our intervention by pointing to Nazi plans for eventual world conquest. [13] The intimation that the Western Hemisphere was in imminent peril can be dismissed as an alarmist technique. The military potential of Germany for undertaking such an overseas expedition was fantastically exaggerated. No documents have been uncovered in Nazi archives to prove that an invasion of North or South America was ever contemplated. [14]

The Christian apologist who wants to justify the course of action our government pursued, and the acquiescence or sanction of the American churches, must resort to other arguments.

Usually the vindicator takes his stand on ideological grounds and insists that the highest interests of mankind were at stake. Even if we were not directly threatened by physical force, he maintains, we could not sit idly by and permit the Nazi tyranny to swallow up the free world. From the economic standpoint it was argued that "you can't do business with Hitler." [15] We would have to compete with "slave labor" and our trade would be stifled. The spectacle of a victorious Germany was painted in the darkest colors. If the Axis powers were triumphant, it would mean the blackout of freedom and the annihilation of Christianity. The idols of German nationalism and racial pride had to be destroyed.

But will this explanation really satisfy the earnest Christian inquirer? Again we find that the case is not as cogent as it might first appear, and that the reasoning behind it is fallacious. A number of vexing questions can be injected to cast doubt upon the validity of this defense for our entry into World War II:

1. How far does the responsibility of the United States extend for the preservation of its way of life? Does it include all countries to which it is bound by ideological or cultural ties? Or even those areas of the earth where we have an economic interest? Can we be expected to go to the assistance of any and every nation that is threatened by an alien "ism"?

2. How many of the noble aims for which we purportedly fought in World War II were actually attained? Were the much-heralded "Four Freedoms" of the Atlantic Charter ever put into practice in the postwar world? What countries are enjoying "liberation" today as a result of our crusade in Europe and Asia? [16]

3. If the defeat of Germany and Japan was essential to world security, how could we conscientiously aid another totalitarian power that had an ideological outlook which was equally contrary to ours? How could we ally ourselves with one dictatorship in order to vanquish another? Did we not help pave the way for the postwar spread of Russian Communism?

Looking back, it is difficult to see what conceivable good was accomplished by our entrance into the war. The war began in 1939 with the German invasion of Poland. Poor, defenseless Poland had to be rescued from the Nazi oppressors! But instead of the promised liberation, she gained only a new domination under the heel of the Kremlin. "How has Poland benefited?" the cynic asks. And we have no answer.

The only clear result of our intervention has been the emergence of the Soviet Union as a formidable world power that fills the West with dismay. On the other hand, if we had preserved a "hands-off" policy, it is quite possible that the two warring totalitarian regimes might have weakened each other into impunity. Even if we assume that Germany and Japan had come out on top, we can suppose that stronger conflicts of interest would have arisen between them than among the countries within the Moscow orbit, which is more highly centralized. Besides, the Nazis and the Fascists would never have had the propaganda resources which are at the disposal of the Communists today. They would not have had the immediately available spy rings which the Communist cells in every country provide.[17] When did the German-American Bund ever produce an Alger Hiss or a Harry Dexter White?

No matter how we look at the world today—geographically, politically, or morally—we would have to be blind indeed to assume that our venture into war has improved it in any way. We can only conclude that one evil was crushed to facilitate the propagation of a greater evil.

In the light of all this, let us return to our original question: Was Christian participation in the Second World War justified? The present writer finds it impossible to respond with an unqualified "yes." We must criticize the American churches for not alerting their members more fully to the deception perpetrated during the prewar years, and for not exerting a greater influence in preserving peace. We believe that the war was only partially, if at all, a struggle between righteousness and unrighteousness. We are obliged to view the position of the conscientious objector in World War II with considerable sympathy, although not convinced that his refusal to bear arms was the best and only form of Christian witness. But no Christian could have engaged in this war, in our opinion, without feeling his own and the Church's complicity in the general guilt. Before America was in the war, his opposition to it should have been firm and unyielding. Of course, after he found himself caught in the actual war situation, he would have had to alter his stand. Whether or not he had contributed to the blunders that had led to war, he was now faced with the fact that the conflagration had erupted. Under such circumstances the individual Christian might have been confronted with a choice in which he could not escape sinning. The Christian combatant could only carry out his assigned duties with a daily prayer for forgiveness as he realized the ambiguity of his position. He would have to admit freely in confession to his God that his country had erred in many respects. We do not believe that Christian soldiers or their churches should have prayed for unqualified American victory in the past world war. Rather, the Christian desire should simply have been for an end to the bloodshed, and for the establishment of a just and durable peace—one which ruled out selfish national interests.

But granted that involvement in a world conflict may oblige the Christian to collaborate with the war effort, does it follow that he must condone whatever strategies are utilized to attain victory? A declaration of war does not abrogate or suspend the commandment "Thou shalt not kill." In wartime, as in peacetime, the Christian is forbidden to inflict physical injury upon his neighbor. Supposedly, he is compelled, as a soldier, to kill or wound some people in order that a greater number may be saved. Even on the battlefield, however, if he is truly cognizant of his Christian witness, he should spare human life wherever possible. He should strive to attain the objective of his military unit with a minimum of casualties on both sides. When prisoners are captured, he should not browbeat them, but treat them with kindness. His example and influence should aim at the prevention of atrocities. When a city is seized, he dare not join in the rape and pillage which is the common deportment of most armies. On this point we might do well to listen to John Gerhard:

> Therefore let curses, blasphemies, lusts, etc., be banished from the camps; even in the capture of cities the blood of the citizens must be spared; when victory is definitely in sight let there be no savagery against the female sex, against helpless old men, against the infants and children; let there be no rapes nor unchastity, no snatching of virgins or mothers, since the divine law, "Thou shalt not commit adultery," knows no exception even in war.[18]

The Christian should also have expostulated against such ghastly brutalities on a larger scale as the use of saturation bombing and the dropping of the first atomic bomb. It is not always easy to apply the definition of "legitimate warfare" to such a massive upheaval as World War II was—to distinguish between the wrong and the rightful use of weapons in all phases of such a conflict. But when it was a foregone conclusion that Germany had lost the war, it was nothing less than barbarous and iniquitous to send squadrons of our planes over German cities to rain down destruction and convert them into burning infernos. Thousands of helpless women and children were cremated while yet alive, in the seething cauldrons that had been their homes. Churches and museums and public buildings were razed to the ground. Heaps of smoldering ruins were visible everywhere. Most horrifying to recall is the mass air raid on Dresden, which was swollen with dense crowds of refugees who had fled in frantic fear before the rape and murder inflicted by the Russian hordes overrunning Silesia. Waves of Allied bombers left the city stifled in a cloud of black smoke. Those who tried to escape were riddled with machine guns. The number of corpses was so enormous that they were burned for weeks on funeral pyres. Estimates as to the total number of casualties have varied from a hundred thousand to a quarter of a million. The excuse tendered, that these tactics would end the war sooner, is hard to accept. The only possible achievement that could be claimed for the Dresden massacre was that it accelerated the Russian advance by a few days. Germany was already prostrate in the path of the invading armies before the most devastating bombings were ordered.[19]

Contrary to Allied propaganda and popular opinion, the indiscriminate bombing of civilians did not begin with the Luftwaffe blitz over England, but with a British air raid on Western Germany on May 11, 1940, which marked "the first deliberate breach of the fundamental rule of civilized warfare that hostilities must only be waged against the enemy combatant forces." [20]

J. M. Spaight, former Principal Secretary of the British Air Ministry, boasted that this was "the splendid decision" which enabled the Allies to win the war. He traced it "to a brainstorm which came to British experts in 1936," and claimed that it was as heroic as the "scorched earth" policy of the Russians because it led to the sacrificial suffering of the populace at Coventry, Birmingham, Sheffield, and Southampton. Hitler, he agreed, only undertook the bombing of the British civilian population reluctantly, as a retaliatory measure. In his opinion, the Nazi dictator would gladly have called a halt to the slaughter at any time.[21]

These same facts were repeated by Air Marshal Sir Arthur Harris, who joined in belittling the Germans for not perceiving that the heavy bomber would be a more effective weapon against civilians than soldiers. When reproached for the inhumanity of this type of warfare, he retorted by quoting a British Government White Paper which estimated that the blockade of Europe by the British Navy between 1914 and 1918 "caused nearly 800,000 deaths," while indiscriminate bombing by the R.A.F. between 1940 and 1945 probably did not kill more than three hundred thousand persons.[22]

What do these disclosures do to the premises upon which many American Christians justified our participation in these bombings? Were the organized churches completely ignorant of the facts? Were they acquiescing to the inexorable demands of war? Or did they lack the moral courage to speak up?

Another issue on which the voice of the churches should have been heard was the unprecedented demand for "unconditional surrender," which built up the German will to resist and prolonged the war.

This was not a provision with political and military implications only. It was a degrading demand that could only violate the self-respect of a nation. It was not only foolhardy; it was immoral. It meant that the Allies were unwilling to offer any peace terms to the enemy, which in the case of Germany might have encouraged a revolt against Hitler. Instead, we insisted that we would settle for nothing less than abject and humiliating surrender.[23] How could a Christian who yearned for love and reconciliation have become a party to such a policy? How could the American churches have refrained from expressing their indignation?

The use of the atomic bomb on Hiroshima and Nagasaki has produced some uneasy consciences also. Measured in terms of the cruel suffering and gruesome deaths which they caused, these violent explosions were far worse than the total number of bombings and atrocities ever attributed to the enemy. Dr. Hachiya's diary, which records the incineration of one of these cities and the carnage which he witnessed, has been called a pathologist's view of hell." [24] Attempts to justify the nefarious action have not been convincing. There is general agreement now that Japan was already defeated and on the verge of surrender before the atomic bombs were dropped. If a few American lives were indeed spared because the war was shortened by several weeks, that can hardly exonerate us, in the Christian evaluation of the situation, for having slaughtered hundreds of thousands of Japanese civilians in one truculent stroke. Even if the atomic bomb had to be used, why could it not first have been detonated on some barren wasteland or uninhabited island near Japan to convince the Japanese of the futility of further resistance? If this warning had been ineffective, one bomb could still have been dropped upon an inhabited site, instead of two. While some leading Humanists were horrified by the atomic bomb,[25] most Christians complacently accepted it as only another instrument of war. By this time the callous indifference to human suffering that had been ingrained in our people by four years of war was evident in the lack of Christian sympathy for the unfortunate victims. . . . What had happened to the eyes of the Church? She preferred to look the other way and see nothing.

On August 6, 1955, forty religious and educational leaders called upon Americans to observe the tenth anniversary of the bombing of Hiroshima as a "day of national repentance." The call was sounded in a statement released by the Fellowship of Reconciliation. The allegation that the use of the bomb was a necessary act of self-defense and an "act of mercy" was flatly denied. The blunt accusation was made:

> We hold that Hiroshima was an abhorrent display of national power and that the national attitude toward it was in large measure composed of self-satisfaction, self-righteousness, and arrogance. . . . In spite of certain qualms and fears, we took pride in being the one nation that had the brains and resources to produce the revolutionary new weapons. . . . There has never been anything like a national repentance for the crime of Hiroshima.[26]

Anyone who wants to uphold the righteousness of our cause in the last war will also have to defend the agreements reached at Yalta and Potsdam. These conferences have been blamed for much of our postwar trouble. American sanction was given to the exploitation of German war prisoners as slave labor in Britain and France, as well as in Russia, after the termination of the war. China's sovereignty over Manchuria was virtually cancelled when Stalin was promised control over its railroads, a predominant interest in its chief port, Dairen, and a naval base at Port Arthur.[27] Only American insistence on pushing the Soviet Union into the Far Eastern fighting led the Russians to raise their price and demand economic hegemony over Manchuria. These concessions posited Russia with a strategic position in China that assured future Communist supremacy there. The tragic division of Korea, and the stalemated war that ravaged the country in 1950–53, may plausibly be traced to the blunders of Yalta.[28]

Another stigma on the Allied record is the postwar betrayal of Poland.

One of the major mistakes of the harshly dictated Versailles Treaty had been the creation of the so-called Polish Corridor. When Hitler's armies invaded Poland in September 1939 to "rectify the wrong," Great Britain and France immediately declared war on Germany. In its early stages the war was described in some quarters as a moral crusade to preserve the territorial borders of Poland. Within a few months, however, the very existence of Poland was ignored by the Allies. During the Soviet occupation of Eastern Poland, ruthless measures were taken to stamp out the national consciousness of the Polish people. One million two hundred thousand persons were deported to Russia. Many of them were consigned to slave-labor camps. Our State Department, which at one time had flatly rejected a proposed Soviet annexation of Polish territory as a violation of the Atlantic Charter, was finally persuaded to acquiesce. We turned our backs on Mikolajczyk and the Polish patriots. In July 1945 our government formally recognized the Soviet-sponsored regime.

Another definitely reprehensible policy adopted to a large extent by our government was the Morgenthau Plan for the economic annihilation of Germany. Territorially, under the plan, East Prussia and part of Silesia were to be sliced away from Germany proper. France was to get the Saar and a considerable area on the left bank of the Rhine. The rest of the country was to be partitioned into North and South German states and an International Zone. The mines in the Ruhr were to be closed. Manufacturing plants were to be dismantled. Reparations were to be extracted by forced German labor outside Germany and the confiscation of German assets in all foreign countries. There were to be controls over Germany's foreign trade and tight restrictions on her capital imports. No wonder the Morgenthau Plan was described as intending to reduce Germany to an agrarian state! It was never fully invoked, but it contributed measurably to the vindictive treatment accorded Germany.[29]

Closely related was the process labeled "denazification," which provided for setting up courts throughout Germany, in charge of German collaborators, and instructing them to demote or punish all those found guilty of having followed Adolf Hitler. Under the National Socialist regime only those who professed allegiance to Nazism had been permitted to hold government posts. Consequently, almost everyone who had taken part in public life could be accused of having had Nazi sympathies. What could be more demoralizing to a defeated country than the spectacle of having every city and village divided against itself by denunciations, betrayals, and perjury? Unless a person could claim that he had joined in some act of opposition to Hitler, he had little chance of staying in the good graces of the conqueror. Frightened by the severe penalties imposed, many Germans were pressed into slandering themselves by confessions of imaginary disloyalty. The ruthless application of "denazification" victimized people who would have been patriotic toward any government simply because they regarded it as their civic duty. The dishonest and cowardly elements in the population were encouraged to come to the foreground and become a new class of collaborators, whose welfare would depend upon their willingness to be traitors to their own countrymen.

Again, what had happened to the Christian conscience during this time? It was undoubtedly dulled by constant exposure to the brutalities of war. Christians should have been taking the lead in a prompt repudiation of the Morgenthau Plan for retaliation.

Yet another culpable postwar action in which our government played a prominent part consisted of the anomalous Nuremberg trials. Not only were actual persons suspected of "war crimes" put on trial, but the German leaders were broadly charged with perpetrating "crimes against humanity," forming a conspiracy to wage aggressive war, and bearing responsibility for "crimes against peace." In the Allied nations there was a widespread popular clamor for retribution. The victors thereupon set up their tribunal and confirmed a guilt which was already predetermined. Some churchmen demanded punishment for the Nazis in the name of justice. Only a few were dubious about the equity of the proceedings.

Many of the accusations levied against Germany would be difficult to substantiate. Some could have been used as recriminations against the victors, also. According to their own definition of a "war crime," the Allies were far from innocent. Early in 1941 Britain had invaded and garrisoned Iceland. Later in the same year she had seized the Azores, the Canaries, and the Cape Verde Islands, all of them neutral territories at the time. In November 1942, Britain and the United States had poured troops into Algeria and French Morocco. President Roosevelt justified the landings by maintaining that otherwise German and Italian troops might have come in and become "a direct threat to America across the comparatively narrow sea from Western Africa. . . ." But the argument of General Jodl, that the masses of Russian troops mobilized on the German border forced the German Army to take aggressive action as a preventive blow, was peremptorily dismissed.[30] British plans to occupy Norway were frustrated when the Germans rushed in ahead of them. If they had been successful, they would have been credited with a masterstroke in preventive warfare; but when it was performed by the enemy, the German claim that it was done "for the purpose of forestalling an imminent Allied landing" was denied.

In October 1955 the press gave only slight notice to the release of a frail, seventy-nine-year-old man from the Spandau Allied Military Prison in Berlin. Bent by arthritis and still not fully recovered from a hernia operation, Admiral Erich Raeder was at last granted his freedom, although he had been sentenced to life imprisonment at Nuremberg for having plotted the German invasion of Norway, in what has been called "the most monstrous of all the miscarriages of justice." [31] The indictment against the German admiral was never withdrawn, in spite of the revelation by Winston Churchill, in his book *The Gathering Storm,* that British naval authorities were making precisely the same plans for an attack on Norway and had taken aggressive action twenty-four hours earlier than the Germans.

Worst of all, and what makes the Nuremberg trials an opprobrious travesty on justice, is the fact that Soviet Russia was permitted to join in making the condemnation and in issuing the verdicts. On every count on which the Nazis were incriminated, their Russian judges could have been found equally guilty, if not more so. In November 1939, without provocation, Russia had declared war on Finland. In June 1940 the Baltic states of Estonia, Latvia, and Lithuania had been forced into the Soviet orbit. At the end of the war Russian armies had swept into Manchuria and North Korea, and converted these lands into satellite states. While German leaders were convicted for violating the borders of Poland, it was hypocritically overlooked that Russia too had invaded and occupied half of that country. With two parties having committed an act alleged to be criminal, we had at Nuremberg the incredible spectacle of one such party being put on trial by the other!

One of the alleged crimes of the Nazis was the mass deportation of persons from occupied territories, with all of its attendant evils, including maltreatment and malnutrition. But this nefarious practice was exactly what the Russians subsequently carried out. There was a mass removal of Poles from Eastern Poland to Russia. Consequently, and as a result of *Allied* decisions, displaced persons swarmed into the Western Zone of Germany. As early as February 1946, it was estimated that altogether some seventeen million persons had been evicted from their homes and deprived of their property, and that twenty and forty million persons were without a roof over their heads. [32]

One specific indictment of the German leaders was for the cold-blooded murder of eleven thousand Polish officers in the Katyn

Forest near Smolensk. The Soviet authorities who pressed the charge did not even bother to fabricate a plausible myth. They blandly asked that a conviction be recorded on the basis of threadbare mendacities. The only witness produced by the prosecution was a Bulgarian professor who had previously examined the mass grave at Katyn, and had signed the unanimous report of the international committee of inquiry that the atrocity had been committed by the Russians. He was brought before the tribunal and reversed his opinion; he had obviously been intimidated. A Swiss professor, Dr. Naville, who might have been called as a readily available witness from a neutral state, was not summoned. The American and British members of the court were placed in an exceedingly embarrassing dilemma. If the Germans had been acquitted of the Katyn massacre, as honesty required it, would have been equivalent to putting the blame on the Russians. So we need not conjecture as to the reason why the international military tribunal preferred to pass over the accusation with a dignified silence.

In the summer of 1948 belated charges were brought against three famous generals, Field Marshal Gerd von Rundstedt, Field Marshal Fritz Erich von Manstein, and Colonel-General Strauss, who had spent the previous three years in honorable captivity in England as prisoners-of-war. A storm of protest rose in Britain, but to no avail. A total of seventeen accusations were made against Manstein. On only two of these points was he declared guilty. The first charge upheld by the court was that he had permitted Russian prisoners to be used in clearing minefields. The second was that he had allowed Russian civilians to be deported from the Eastern Front for work in Germany. Compared with the gravity of the original indictment, the offenses of which the Field Marshal was found guilty seemed relatively insignificant. Nevertheless, the sixty-two-year-old, half-blind soldier was solemnly informed that he must serve eighteen years in prison for his war crimes.[33]

The simulation and injustice of these proceedings become apparent when we are compelled to admit that on every count on which the vanquished were condemned, the victors were also guilty. For example, German prisoners of war were used to clear away minefields—a practice for which Manstein was held accountable. While Allied tribunals were passing judgment on the German use of forced Russian labor, it was common knowledge that many thousands of civilians from Eastern Germany and the Baltic countries were languishing in Siberian concentration camps.[34]

While the high-ranking Nazis were being condemned for "crimes" of which their judges were equally guilty, and under an authority and jurisdiction that had no basis whatever in international law, American Christians were either applauding or saying nothing. Only an occasional intrepid soul had the temerity to object. There were, most likely, many Christians who felt restive in the face of the tragic farce, but they did not dare to speak up.

In the treatment of prisoners-of-war, also, this held true, as the trials reached another low point in moral turpitude. The abusive maltreatment of German war captives, when it became widely publicized after the war, incited protests from various quarters. The British, French, and Americans had often practiced great cruelty in their P.O.W. camps. Commanding officers had refused to grant medical attention to sick prisoners. In interrogation camps unconvicted suspects had been left naked in unheated cells and forced to perform nauseating menial tasks. Leonard O. Mosley reported from Belsen at the time that camp was put under British guard:

> The British soldiers . . . beat the S.S. guards and set them to collecting the bodies of the dead, keeping them always at the double. . . . When one of them dropped to the ground with exhaustion, he was kicked until he ran again, or prodded with a bayonet, to the accompaniment of lewd shouts and laughs. When one tried to escape, or disobeyed an order, he was shot. . . . The punishment these guards got was in the best Nazi tradition, and few of them survived it.[35]

Prisoners who failed to confess to alleged war crimes were severely beaten, sometimes to the point of unconsciousness. One former American who had collaborated with the Fascists was captured in Italy and driven insane by his tormentors before he could be put on trial. That the German armies practiced unnecessary cruelties, no one can deny. But we lapse into Pharisaism if we imagine that American armies were always under well-disciplined control and circumspect in their behavior. Man's inhumanity to man is not limited to one nationality. War breeds hatred and ferocity. Who has been so cloistered from grim realities that he has heard nothing of the barbarities perpetrated by our own troops?

The author recalls all too vividly the shock which he received when one serviceman told him how American soldiers took their Japanese prisoners, blindfolded them, and forced them to jump off a precipitous cliff. Such premeditated murder was "justified" on the grounds that their enemies in the Orient were savages who did not deserve to be classified as members of the human race.

An American officer related the story of how his company captured a number of Germans, took them for a "walk," and caused them to "disappear." Because of the mood of vengeance which prevailed, he deemed it the better part of valor not to interfere.

A Chicago churchman tells of visiting a German minister now serving the cause of the Gospel in Egypt. During the war the German pastor was conscripted into the *Wehrmacht* and was taken to the United States as an American prisoner. For the rest of his life he will retain an unsolicited memento of his "visit" here. A drunken American soldier took the liberty of carving his initials on the German *Pfarrer's* back with a bayonet.

And these are not just a few isolated instances! Many more could be put into the record to match the atrocities attributed to the Nazis and the Japs. Only ignorance or hypocrisy can account for American clergymen's stepping into their pulpits to denounce the evils of Hitlerism while preserving a discreet silence in regard to the sins of their own government and their own armed forces.

To summarize our disillusionment regarding the Second World War, we need only compare the objectives proclaimed by our wartime President with the results attained. In the lofty pronouncements of the Atlantic Charter, Roosevelt and Churchill declared that they were opposed to any territorial changes that would not be in accord "with the freely expressed wishes of the peoples concerned." They promised to "respect the right of all peoples to choose the form of government under which they will live," and they said that they wanted independence restored to all those nations that had been forcibly deprived of their sovereign rights.

These glittering generalities became meaningless as the war progressed. Collaboration with the Soviet Union and the demand for unconditional capitulation made the joint statement of the wartime leaders a worthless document, foredoomed to the ash heap. Even before the war ended, it was announced that the Atlantic Charter did not apply to Germany. The "sell-out" at Yalta and Potsdam was the logical outcome of the nefarious alliance with Communism which made peace with honor an impossibility.

What about Christians reactions to our conflict with Communism in the Far East? The American churches never seemed to come to grips with some of the moral issues posed by the war in Korea: Could intervention in that part of Asia rightfully be called a defensive action? If so, how could we avoid prosecuting the war to a successful conclusion? As a military leader, MacArthur submitted that "there is no substitute for victory." The time-honored tradition of a just war as defined by theologians has usually included the indispensable condition that there be a reasonable prospect for victory. The dismissal of MacArthur overruled any likelihood of attaining more than the limited objective of an armistice which would leave the country divided and only strengthen the forces of Communism for future aggression. Knowing that the stalemate would be prolonged, and that we had no clearly defined war aim, how could the American clergy have encouraged the youth of their churches to participate in the conflict with a clear conscience? Just where was the consistency in an American policy which demanded absolute victory with a vengeance over Nazism, but which was willing to be bogged down with a bloody and inconclusive struggle with Communism? Just how did the Korean War meet the standards usually set up for a just war?

Much was made of the cruelty of the North Koreans, as though there were suddenly some innate distinction between them and the inhabitants of the southern part of the peninsula, in whose interest the war was avowedly fought. We should be appalled, then, when we read this report of a British war correspondent: "Around Seoul the execution squads of Syngman Rhee had begun to work so feverishly and ferociously at their murderous tasks that a great wave of indignation swept through all those who saw and heard. Men and women [and even children, it was reliably written] were dragged from the prisons of Seoul, marched to fields on the outskirts of the town, and shot carelessly and callously in droves and shovelled into trenches." [36]

Who won in Korea? The Communists claimed that they had been triumphant. Malenkov sent a telegram to the North Korean Premier calling the armistice "a great victory for the Korean Army and the Chinese People's Volunteers." The Peking radio echoed the same jubilant report.

Those who defended the Korean adventure maintained that the record proved otherwise. Since the original purpose of the Communist invasion had been to conquer the whole of Korea, our spokesmen claimed that they had not achieved their goal. We were "consoled" with a recital of the enormous number of casualties inflicted on the enemy. The Communist armies were said to have suffered about two million casualties, and of the ten million people who had been living in North Korea, one out of every three had died as a result of the hostilities. Thousands of Communist prisoners refused to return to their homeland, so we took comfort in the loss of face incurred by the Communists.

Upon sober reflection, we may wonder whether some of this is not wishful thinking. Has our intervention accomplished much of lasting value? If the U.N. had not interfered when it did, the entire peninsula would have fallen into Communist hands, but what guarantee do we have that this will not be the ultimate fate of the country anyway? Have we really promoted a desire on the part of the people in the Far East to withstand Communism? The writer must admit that he was dubious in 1953, and he is even more dubious now.

Hostilities broke out in Indo-China soon after World War II, when France attempted to re-establish control over the Associated States of Indo-China—Vietnam, Cambodia, and Laos. On November 27, 1946, six French warships shelled a defenseless city, killing six thousand men, women, and children. In the early stages of the war the rebels seemed more nationalist than Communist. But with the Kremlin, as usual, exploiting the hunger and misery of oppressed peoples, it became possible for the Reds to pose as the champions of the forces seeking freedom from Western colonialism. The French soon became weary of a war which cost them a terrific price in blood and treasure. Still, they stubbornly refused to take the crucial step which might have saved the country from Communism—the granting of complete independence. The concessions that finally were made to the Vietnamese were too little and too late. By 1954 the United States was bearing nearly eighty per cent of the financial burden necessary to continue the war. The hard truth was that military victory was impossible without United States intervention, and even then it was doubtful unless the Indo-Chinese could be persuaded that they had something worth fighting to achieve. Without clarifying our objectives, some top leaders in our Administration began beating the war drums in 1953 in a whirlwind effort to break down popular resistance to the idea of sending American soldiers to Indo-China.

In the face of this threat of embroilment in an alien war, in which we would be abetting the preservation of a colonial empire by a European country pretending to have a power which it no longer really possessed, the Christian conscience was strangely subdued. Few churchmen warned against the serious implications of a blundering American foreign policy which opposed a negotiated settlement without offering a reasonable alternative.

No sensible person would deny that there are and always have been numerous tyrannical governments running rampant in the world. Witness the startling revelations of corruption following the collapse of the Peron regime in Argentina! But the disturbing question arises whether *every* evil which appears on the international horizon can and should be extirpated by force. Can either the United States or the United Nations extinguish every flame of iniquity that arises in some remote corner of the earth? The task, if it were really to be undertaken, would be too immense for achievement. Besides, the temptation is always to ignore those injustices which do not directly threaten our own security. And does not every attempt to destroy the "wicked enemy" result in a degradation of the "innocent accuser"? Captain Russell Grenfell puts it this way: "Moral indignation at another nation's expense is nearly always injudicious. Kaiser Wilhelm's scorn over Britain's behavior to the Boers was soon returned sevenfold over the German violation of Belgian neutrality, while the recent sanguinary episodes in United Nations Korean prisoner-of-war camps were not a happy aftermath to numerous executions of Germans by the victors in the war for much the same thing." [37]

This book does not pretend to cover all of the criticisms that might be directed against the conduct of the American churches in the Second World War and its aftermath.[38] Those that have been advanced, however, should suffice for stimulating contrition and self-reproach. May the confession of our past mistakes guide us toward improvement in the future as we strive to "be blameless and harmless, the sons of God, without rebuke, in the midst of a crooked and perverse nation," shining "as lights in the world, holding forth the word of life" (Phil. 2:15–16).

5

~~~~~~~~~~~~~~~~~~~~~~~~~~~~~~~~~~~~~

The Problematic Future: The Christian and Hydrogen Warfare

Without even contemplating the horrors anticipated in the hydrogen warfare of the future, we must admit that modern wars have already degenerated to a level of incredible savagery. History shows that there have always been "wars and rumors of wars," as far back as we can trace the story of man. The intermittent conflicts that have flared up during past ages have always resulted in death or misery for many people. But the barbarism exhibited by both sides in the Second World War was so extreme that we are hard pressed to find historical parallels to it.

At various times efforts have been made to "humanize" war. Even the ancient Hebrews had a reputation for mercy, according to the Syrians.[1] There were restrictions on inter-Christian warfare in the Middle Ages, even if there were none on wars against pagans. The Truce of God placed church buildings, monks, pilgrims, merchants, and women outside the bounds of war. The Geneva Convention tried to define rules of civilized warfare, and included the provision that a prisoner-of-war was to be given a fair trial.

To find comparisons with the infamous deeds of our generation of warriors, we would have to turn our attention back to a figure like King Tiglath Pileser of Assyria, who recorded that he captured a city and "piled high the heads of the inhabitants before the gates thereof"—and this practice of erecting a pyramid of human skulls was duplicated by the medieval Tartar conqueror Tamerlane. But a similar result was achieved through the bombing of Dresden in 1945:

So enormous were the number of bodies that nothing
could be done but to pile them on timber collected from
the ruins and there to burn them. In the *Altmarkt* one
funeral pyre after another disposed of five hundred bodies
or parts of bodies at a time.[2]

F. J. P. Veale is unwilling to credit Christianity with any "per-
ceptible practical influence in mitigating the barbarous conduct of
war." Willing to overlook the cruelties of the Franklin and Gothic
kings who had nominally embraced Christianity, he reminds us that
the devout Byzantine emperors conducted their wars with the same
ferocity that characterized the warrior kings of the Orient. For
example, a ruler by the name of Basil made it a practice in his campaigns against the Bulgarians to put out the eyes of his prisoners,
on one occasion blinding as many as fifteen thousand men. The
Albigensian Crusade of 1209, designed to root out heresy in France,
was directed by one of the greatest of the popes, Innocent III. A
contemporary observer estimated that five hundred thousand people perished. One of the most protracted and devastating conflicts
of all time was waged in the name of religion—the Thirty Years
War (1618–1648). "It has been calculated that the population of
Bohemia was reduced from three million to eight hundred thousand. . . . For more than a generation after the war, one-third of
the arable land in North Germany remained uncultivated." Some
twenty-five thousand people were massacred at Magdeburg in 1631,
"not one in fifty of whom was armed." [3]

Of course, it may be argued that when "civilized warfare" became the general practice in Europe, its acceptance was restricted
to "Christian" nations. Whether it had any direct relationship to
Christian influences is a debatable question. The fact remains that
the non-Western world continued to fight with the unrestricted
ferocity that had been usual in ancient times. When Nadir Shah
invaded India in 1739, he was no less barbarous than Asshurbanipal
had been when he invaded Elam. When the Turks suppressed the
revolt of the Greeks in 1821, or the revolt of the Bulgarians in 1876,
they applied the same violent methods as we would expect the
Persians under King Darius to have used. But the code developed
among European countries that hostilities between civilized peo-

ples must be limited to the armed forces actually engaged in combat. A careful distinction was drawn between combatants and noncombatants. From the beginning of the eighteenth century down to the Second World War, European "civil wars" were generally fought according to comparatively humane rules. Often the profession of the soldier was a rather safe one. Military campaigns were sometimes conducted with scarcely any loss of life. Disease and lack of sanitation accounted for more death than did the weapons of war. The moderation advocated by the Age of Reason carried over into military life. Wars were fought with limited means and for limited objectives. Even when weapons became more powerful and accurate, civilians were supposed to be exempted from their deadly effects.

With the outbreak of the French Revolution, international warfare in Europe entered upon a new phase. The epoch of kings' wars gave way to the era of peoples' wars. Large mass armies were raised by conscription and wars became more lethal. Propaganda against the enemy was professionally engineered to whip up public enthusiasm for fighting. Already in the Napoleonic wars the loss of life vastly exceeded that in conflicts like the Seven Years War.

The American Civil War marked a considerable departure from the tactics that had been previously associated with civilized warfare. Although General Robert E. Lee was faithful to the European code and a perfect example of military chivalry, General Ulysses S. Grant is said to have grasped the concept of total war and realized that the destruction of the economic resources of the South would be the way to victory. General Sherman, who conducted the ignominious march through Georgia, adopted this policy to the fullest extent. After expelling the inhabitants of Atlanta from their homes, he systematically demolished the factories and mills of the city. After laying waste some of the richest lands of the South, he expressed his determination to capture Charleston. "The whole army," he wrote to General Halleck in Washington, "is burning with insatiable desire to wreak vengeance upon South Carolina." [4] Sherman's belief, which he carried into practice, that war is hell and cannot be mollified may now be seen as a historical precedent for the utter disregard for civilian life that characterized World

War II, and which would be one of the most ghastly aspects of all-out atomic warfare in our own time.

Before World War I, Admiral Lord Fisher advocated the maxim "Hit first, hit hard, and hit anywhere." When the German naval-building program threatened British supremacy on the high seas, he begged for permission to end the armament race by taking his battleships over to Kiel and sinking the whole German fleet in a surprise attack on the harbor. When Germany adopted unrestricted submarine warfare in 1917, he refused to join the chorus of denunciation. Humanitarian scruples were weakening drastically everywhere. Much damage was done to French and Belgian cities as a result of German artillery bombardments. But the worst onslaught upon civilian life came with the British blockade of Germany, which led to the starvation of nearly a million noncombatants. By 1919, when the question of war indemnities arose, it was clearly understood that war had become fabulously costly. And the bereavements which left vacant spots in so many European homes were painful reminders of the increasing toll in young lives demanded by modern warfare.

With the Second World War came "the splendid decision" to indulge in the indiscriminate bombing of civilians. Weapons of all kinds became ever more powerful. The Germans experimented with rocket-propelled missiles. Finally the announcement was made that atomic bombs had been dropped upon Hiroshima and Nagasaki. Combined with the horrible new modes of warfare was the policy of vengeance which called for unconditional surrender and led to the infamous war trials. By 1945 the cycle was complete. Man could boast of his "advance" to the "highest level" of barbarism.

Churches which have advocated or at least permitted Christian participation in past wars may be compelled to reconsider their position as we plunge ahead into the atomic era. Even the thesis that a war may possibly be the lesser of two evils is hard to maintain when we are confronted with the prospect of total annihilation.

Many scientists of good will and great learning worked on the difficult assignment of developing the atom bomb. Yet some declined to collaborate in a scientific quest which they suspected might become a sinister enterprise. Some who had previously been inclined to deny that science had any moral implications were suddenly stirred by the tragic potentialities inherent in uncontrolled atomic weapons. Physicists who had been uninterested in any discussion of ethics emerged from the secluded atmosphere of their laboratories to become crusaders for peace. Like lonely prophets they issued warnings of possible annihilation unless adequate safeguards could be set up. Even those whose titanic efforts had given birth to this new weapon were not sure whether they had played midwife to prodigy or monster. Norman Cousins called the achievement of the scientists "victory tempered by primitive fear . . . fear of the unknown." [5] Sumner Welles wrote in the *Atlantic Monthly*: "The unleashing of atomic power [has] blackened the world with a poisonous fog of suspicion and fear. The atomic bomb has touched all peoples with hysteria." [6]

The moral reactions to the dropping of the atomic bomb from non-ecclesiastical sources make interesting comparisons with those emanating from the churches. Strangely enough, the secular press showed more moral concern than some contributors to the religious press. *Time* Magazine commented on August 20, 1945:

> The race had been won, the weapon had been used by those on whom civilization could best hope to depend; but the demonstration of power against living creatures instead of dead matter created a bottomless wound in the living conscience of the race. . . . When the bomb split open the universe . . . it . . . revealed the oldest, simplest, commonest, most neglected and most important of facts: that each man is eternally and above all else responsible for his own soul, and, in the terrible words of the Psalmist, that no man may deliver his brother, nor make agreement unto God for him. [7]

Less than a week after Hiroshima had been demolished by atomic fires, Robert M. Hutchins denounced the act in a broadcast from the University of Chicago. If the bomb had to be used at all, he insisted, it should have been only as a last resort in self-defense. In a University of Chicago Round Table broadcast on November 11, 1945, he deplored the "policy of force" which he said had been officially adopted by the United States:

One of the most distressing aspects of this policy is the air of moral superiority with which we state it. Mr. Truman hints that we are entitled to world domination because we are devoted to the Ten Commandments and the Golden Rule. But it is a little difficult to see how dropping atomic bombs, without warning, upon the men, women and children of Hiroshima and Nagasaki could have been suggested to us by either the Ten Commandments or the Golden Rule.[8]

Since 1945 we have moved into the atomic era at an accelerated pace. The bombs used on Japan seem like toys compared with the monstrous H-bombs which have been tested in experiments since then. More so than in connection with the A-bomb, the feeling has been expressed that making the H-bomb is clearly immoral. Even Dr. Teller, who pressed hard for completing the H-bomb, was later uneasy about the result. When asked in 1954 how we could preserve a reasonable degree of happiness in a world where aggressive weapons had become so powerful, he was unable to suggest an answer.[9]

When Gordon Dean, Chairman of the United States Atomic Energy Commission from 1950 to 1953, wrote his report in book form, he admitted the fact that a hydrogen bomb could be deliberately rigged with materials that would become highly radioactive after exploding. The deadly particles would be disseminated into the atmosphere and over the surface of the earth for thousands of miles in the direction of the prevailing winds. All living things which they encountered would be destroyed.

> The prudence, or even the military value, of such an inhumane device would be open to serious question, even for one obsessed with the mad dream of world conquest. Used in this way, the H-bomb would not be a weapon of war; it would be an instrument for the destruction of civilization and possibly of all mankind.[10]

One of the most severe jolts to Western security came in August 1953, with the announcement that the Russians had succeeded in making a thermonuclear bomb. Extremely disconcerting to those whose hopes for peace have been anchored on atomic superiority has been the revelation that Russia is gradually catching up with our larger stockpile of bombs. Almost simultaneously has come the realization that Russia will be able to deliver such bombs with long-range bombers or possibly intercontinental rockets. Our complacency is thoroughly shattered when we are told that America is far more vulnerable to attack than the Soviet Union, since our industries are concentrated in a number of cities which would make excellent targets, while the Russians have deliberately spread theirs over an area of eight million square miles. The Civil Defense Administration's test of June 1954 assumed that nine million people could or would be killed in an H-bomb attack. Sociologist Hornell Hart speaks of two and a half million casualties, but this does not include the probable effects of panic and anarchy.[11]

The magazine *United States News and World Report* has offered its readers a close insight into the latest atomic weapons on the basis of an interview with Donald A. Quarles, Head of Research for the Armed Forces.[12] Push-button warfare seems to be more than a dream, this report suggested. The comic-strip fantasies associated with Buck Rogers or Flash Gordon are becoming realities. Mr. Quarles stated that the atomic bomb used at the end of World War II was in a "primitive form" which has now "been enormously refined and developed and exploited for a great variety of uses, rather than for particular strategic-bombing use as it was then conceived."

In the field of guided missiles we are informed that "we are passing beyond the physical limitations of a man in performance requirements. . . ." Altogether "there are two or three dozen kinds of guided missiles," with individual names such as "Nike" and "Terrier." The German V-1 was only a "primitive" weapon, and the once-formidable V-2 may now be looked upon as only the forerunner of a much more dangerous family of weapons.

Missiles travel today at speeds all the way from somewhat below the velocity of sound (as in the case of the pilotless bomber called "The Matador") "up to perhaps twenty times the velocity of sound." Missiles equipped with rocket motors can travel five thousand miles in a matter of thirty or forty minutes. (This would be five or six times the speed of a high-powered rifle bullet. These are the so-called ballistic missiles, which reach their maximum velocity shortly after launching and thereafter travel as free-flying or free-falling bodies.)

A cautious answer has been given to the questions, "Is not the terrible age still quite a way off, and is there any assurance that these dreadful weapons would really succeed?" Although the completion and perfection of some of the weapons now envisioned may not be possible within the near future, "the art is being pushed forward."

The *Nautilus* is in operation with an atomic power plant, and more advanced power plants are being developed for submarine propulsion. The atomic cannon is said to look like a valuable weapon for future wars.

If this is not enough to fill us with apprehension, we are further informed that both East and West have nerve gases available that would be toxic and dangerous. Specifically, "there is a particular kind of poison that attacks the nerve centers and causes a paralysis which, in turn, causes death. As compared with the poison gases used in the First World War, the nerve gases have peculiar properties that make them lethal in small doses."

Let the question be asked: "What about air defenses—the radar screen and things of that kind? Are they effective?" The answer must be: "Yes. However, even with warnings and improved defensive weapons, it will still be a very difficult problem to intercept and destroy all or even a very large fraction of the planes that might come over in a mass attack." We should not be deluded into thinking that we can have an airtight defense. Work for peace from a position of strength—this is the only advice that Mr. Quarles has to contribute for avoiding war.[12]

The cost of preparing to wage atomic warfare has risen to astronomical proportions. The monetary expenditures necessary for maintaining our Armed Forces stagger the imagination. At the beginning of the 1956 fiscal year, which started July 1, 1955, it was estimated that the Federal Government would spend $63,800,000,-000. Of that figure, 60.8 percent would go for current military purposes, 10.7 percent for interest on the national war debt, and 7.5 percent for veterans' services and benefits. The cost of present and past wars amounts to over three fourths of the government's total outlay of funds.[13]

The stupendous cost of producing atomic weapons, coupled with the dread of their destructive power, has led some optimists to presume that war is now less likely than before. It has been argued that the urgency of the problem facing the whole of mankind will forge a new unity among the divided peoples of the world. Some spokesmen go so far as to suggest that the Atomic Age will be a new Utopia. Dr. Vannevar Bush has made the bold assertion that "the atom bomb means the end of world war. . . . Fear will prevent it."[14] The Christian who has a more realistic understanding of human nature knows how absurd this expectation is. The atom's fury is no guarantee in itself that man will apply it to constructive purposes.

A military expert like Lieutenant-Colonel F. O. Miksche flatly rejects the theory of "peace through fear" as wishful thinking. He writes:

> There is unfortunately little reason to believe that A-bombs, by the mere fact of their existence and the horror implicit in them, will avert war. . . . War has always been a phenomenon so closely bound up with human life that it would almost appear to be a necessity and a biological law.

It is Mr. Miksche's prediction that if belligerents were to use only tactical A-weapons in the beginning of any future war, it is still likely that the conflict would develop by degrees into a strategical air war. A gradual transformation toward more violent forms is a "natural evolution usual in wars."[15]

Dr. Arthur H. Compton, who played a leading role in the development of atomic power, says that "wars are not yet obsolete, but they are obsolescent." The likelihood of atomic retaliation against any aggressor *should* serve as a deterrent against the instigation of war. The increasing interdependence of individuals and groups within the social order *ought* to be an effective guarantee against a disruption of that order. Yet Dr. Compton admits that his hopes for peace during the next decade rest primarily on the preservation of a balance of power between the United States and Russia. If the Communists should attain military superiority, he maintains, he would be surprised if they did not exert whatever pressure was necessary to bring the world under their control.[16] An uncertain stalemate in the race for atomic superiority is not the secure foundation on which we would like to base our hopes for peace.

The magnificent scientific mind of man has brought him to the brink of self-destruction. Prince Louis de Broglie, Secretary of the French Academy of Science and Nobel Prize-winning physicist, warned in 1954 that enough hydrogen bombs had already been exploded to create serious dangers for the world's animal and plant life. He declared that the physical phenomena already produced had outstripped the capability of scientists to calculate their ultimate effect.[17] Two University of Illinois professors have asserted that a hydrogen-bomb war could start a "creeping suicide" that might wipe mankind from the earth one thousand years hence. "The real threat from the use of H-bomb," they have said, "is the danger of long-range damage to the hereditary endowment of the human race." Whole nations might be exposed to persistent radioactivity, with the result that the number of people with mental disorders and high susceptibility to disease—the genetically unfit— would be multiplied.[18] Admitting that there is still considerable uncertainty about the actual effects of nuclear weapons upon heredity, Harold Miller foresees that "our present war preparations will produce effects on future generations who will be carrying on human civilization long after our present quarrels are forgotten." [19]

The prediction is openly made today (1956) that within a year or less the United States or Russia will be able to test an intercontinental missile capable of carrying the H-bomb. Traveling at three times the speed of a rifle bullet, it would presumably soar 600 miles into the stratosphere, and then descend on a target thousands fo miles away, too fast for any known means of interception to stop it. Many are fearful that Russia is winning the missile race.

Already now the United States is spending, for research and on the development of such missiles, at the rate of a billion dollars a year.[20]

We live in a nightmare world. We hear that the hydrogen bomb is not the end of the race in nuclear weapons. Since the spring of 1954 there have been rumors and reports about the cobalt bomb, which would be so lethal that it could not even be tested. All that would be necessary to make the C-bomb, we are told, is to wrap in a sheath of cobalt those H-bombs which have already been tested. Then we would have a bomb whose deadly emission of radioactivity could keep circling the globe for years and years, until all life was extinct.

Christians who are novices in science and who know little about atomic power cannot speak from first-hand acquaintance about the magnitude of these frightening weapons. Yet they cannot help but share the anxiety of the authorities who *are* in a position to know, and who make the most dire predictions. Sir Robert Robinson, President of the British Association for the Advancement of Science, is still not sure that a hydrogen bomb will not "set fire to the lighter elements and blow up the earth."[21]

More and more it becomes questionable whether the Christian ethics which were contrived to meet war situations that arose in A.D. 800 or 1600 can be applied to the Atomic Age. Can the definitions and moral judgments of Thomas Aquinas or Martin Luther or John Calvin be regarded as authoritative for a type of warfare which was beyond their wildest dreams but which confronts the Christian today as stark reality? How many of our theological minds are really grappling with the problem of the Christian's relationship to a war which can have no conceivable objective that is worth fighting for? Is it possible to endorse an atomic war in any degree or in any sense? Some time ago an editorial in the *Christian Century* sounded the alarm: "This is the end of the line. The road runs no farther. The desperate race for atomic power has reached its ultimate goal. Almost before our finite minds could take it in, we have leaped from the speculative formula to the threshold of extinction."[22] Where now, world? Where do we go from here, Christian theologians?

In a minority report for the Anglican Committee on the Church and the Atom, the Archdeacon of Stoke-on-Trent wrote:

> I suggest that the whole conception of the just war should be abandoned and that the Church should start with the actual facts of modern war and consider them *de novo* in the light of the New Testament revelation of the character of the will of God.[23]

During the Second World War the Federal Council of the Churches of Christ in America called upon a group of theologians to prepare a statement on the attitude of the Christian Church toward the war. They agreed that

> We should begin with an act of contrition. As American Christians, we are deeply penitent for the irresponsible use already made of the atomic bomb. We are agreed that, whatever be one's judgment of the ethics of war in principle, the surprise bombings of Hiroshima and Nagasaki are morally indefensible.[24]

In April 1954 the Archbishop of York used a TV broadcast to implore that the three great powers decide on a plan for controlling the bomb, to dispel "an atmosphere of paralyzing insecurity." The International Affairs Commission of the National Christian Council of Japan expressed "uneasiness" over the H-bomb tests in the Pacific, and called upon the churches of the world to cooperate in promoting international control of atomic power for peace. The service agencies of the Mennonites, the Church of the Brethren, and the Quakers issued a joint Good Friday 1954 statement about the H-bomb:

> Let us be done with these fearful weapons, regardless of what others do . . . for mankind in 1954 the Cross of Christ stands in the shadow of the cross of hydrogen.[25]

Religious leaders in Chicago joined a number of business men and educators in making an urgent appeal to President Eisenhower to cancel the proposed H-bomb tests in the spring of 1956. In their statement, prepared under the auspices of the American Friends Service Committee, they objected to the contamination of plant and animal life that would result, and they argued that it would be senseless to intensify the menace which these weapons already held for mankind. They pleaded that the Pacific bomb tests be deferred and a serious effort be made to seek agreement with Russia on the cessation of bomb tests.[26]

Early in 1956 it was revealed that the Pentagon had distributed a textbook, *Your Life Plans and the Armed Forces*,[27] to every high school in the nation. It was recommended that a six-week unit in eleventh-grade English or social science be taught in which use could be made of the material provided in the textbook. Military conscription is regarded in this textbook as a permanent feature of our society, and armed might is set forth as our great hope in combating Communism. A military career is glamorized and a period of duty in the armed forces is described as a desirable educational experience. Progress toward mature living is to be achieved, according to this attractive account, through religious activities, sports, the use of libraries, and foreign travel. Nothing is said about the moral temptations that have proved overpowering to many servicemen, or about the prospect of American involvement in a suicidal war that would be waged for a dubious cause. Shall this trend toward permanent militarism go unchecked? What shall the churches say and do about conscription for a nuclear war?

The Christian leaders of our country must address themselves in public sermons and private counseling to the perplexed Christians who seek some clarification of the stand they should take in the current confusion seemingly ever worse confounded. Disturbed young consciences, faced with conscription into military service, are searching for advice. Does the commandment "Thou shalt not kill" lose all meaning during wartime? Can we concede that atomic weapons and mass slaughter are legitimate while we contend that the murder of one civilian alone, in peacetime, may justify the death penalty for the murderer? Perhaps some felon condemned to the electric chair may reiterate to his prison chaplain the protest of Roskolnikov in Dostoyevsky's *Crime and Punishment*, that the blood which he has shed is that "which all men shed, which flows and has always flowed in streams, which is spilt like champagne, and for which men are crowned in the capitol, and are called afterwards benefactors of mankind." [28]

To be sure, if we were really interested in following a consistent policy, and if the grounds on which we went to war against Germany and Japan were justified, we would be obliged to invade Russia at once and demand the unconditional surrender of the Soviet leaders. All of the evils which we associated with Nazism and Japanese nationalism are more glaringly prevalent in the Union of Soviet Socialist Republics. The ideological conflict between Communism and Christianity is much more clear today than the opposition between Christianity and the Axis powers ever was. We may rightfully charge Communism with being atheistic and materialistic. We know that its conception of the unimportance of human life has caused it to enslave people and use them as mere means to economic ends.

But we are not likely to defeat this rival way of life by a "war of righteousness." Christians dare not permit a war for world domination to be camouflaged as a Christian crusade against atheism. We should have learned by our experience in the last two world wars that the surest way to spread Communism is to attempt to defeat it by military force. Although we must resist intrigue and suppress insurrection when they threaten us, we must reject war as an instrument for achieving good in the world. A "preventive war" against Communism should be unthinkable to the Christian. When we pause to ponder the perils of atomic warfare, we may well say even more—we may express a legitimate doubt that war can possibly have *any* meaning in terms of right and wrong.

There is no reason to live in a fool's paradise and think that "the spirit of Geneva" indicates a basic change in Soviet policy or long-range ambitions. Although it is too early at this writing to assess the full implications of the anti-Stalin campaign, only the unwary will accept at its face value the "new look" being promulgated by the Russian leaders. There have been so many changes in the party line which have only been tactical maneuvers that it is hard to believe that the latest shift is a real and final retreat from the aim of world conquest for Communism. But no matter how gloomy the outlook, the true Christian never despairs. Believing that God is the Lord of history, he always looks for a ray of hope. It is barely possible that in due time the ideology of Russian Communism will be modified or that eventually a revolution will occur within the Soviet Union which will make a reconciliation between the East and the West feasible. More likely still is the consideration that a nuclear war would be so suicidal that it will become necessary for Communists to repudiate, permanently and unequivocally, the Leninist-Stalinist thesis of an inevitable war with the capitalist world.[29]

We must guard against the heresy which presumes that if the evil of Communism were destroyed, there would be no more evil left in the world. This supposition fails to take into account the diabolical element in human nature and the complexity of the evil forces rampant in the world.

It is outside the scope of this book to advise the Christian churches how they can cope with the atomic threat or how they can help guide the nations to peace. There have been many pronouncements on this subject, and we may hope that further studies and evaluations will be made. In these pages we have attempted only to review the performance of representative American denominations in the Second World War and its aftermath, so that Christian thinkers and church leaders will be in a better position to view the Christian conscience on trial. We have perhaps magnified the problem and sharpened the issues, but merely to demonstrate that no easy and superficial solution will be adequate.

We pray that the recognition of our many failures as individual Christians and, collectively, as American church denominations will lead us to repentance, that in the present crisis we will display better judgment and discernment than we have in the past, and that in the years ahead we will echo ever more clearly the voice of the Prince of Peace.

Notes

~~~~~~~~~~~~~~~~~~~~~~~~~~~~~~~~

Chapter 1

1. Quoted by Arthur F. Steinke, *The Bible and War* (Brooklyn, Studio Press, 1941), p. 18.
2. Kirby Page in *Jesus or Christianity*, quoted by Steinke, *op. cit.*, p. 18.
3. Unless otherwise specified, all Old Testament Biblical quotations are from *An American Translation* (Chicago: University of Chicago Press, 1939).
4. Archaeological research in Palestine is said to have yielded ample evidence of moral corruption among the Canaanites.
5. Cf. II Chron. 18:31. When Jehosaphat was encircled in a battle with the Syrians, he "cried out, and the Lord helped him," while the disguised King of Israel was detected and fatally wounded.
6. Psa. 18. Cf. Psa. 144:1: "Blessed be the Lord, my Rock, who trains my hands for war, my fingers for battle."
7. Cf. Deut. 9:1–14: ". . . never say to yourselves, 'It is because of my goodness that the Lord brought me into possession of this land.' . . . for you are a stiff-necked people."
8. Guy F. Hershberger, "Peace and War in the Old Testament," in *The Mennonite Quarterly Review*, January 1943, p. 22.
9. Hershberger, *op. cit.*, pp. 21–22.

Chapter 2

1. Colonel Gynther Storaasli, "War and Peace," *The Lutheran Chaplain*, January-March 1951, pp. 22–28.
2. Unless otherwise specified, all New Testament references are taken from the Revised Standard Version.
3. Cf. the Presbyterian Confession of Faith in Boettner, *The Christian Attitude Toward War* (Grand Rapids: Eerdmans Publishing Co., 1940), p. 42.
4. Cf. *Lutheran Witness*, August 18, 1942, where these instances are cited to defend the military profession.
5. Translation by John Oman in *On Religion, Speeches to Its Cultured Despisers* (London: 1893), p. 244.
6. Cf. Jamieson, Fausset and Brown, *Commentary on the Whole Bible* (Grand Rapids: Zondervan), Vol. II, p. 123.
7. Cf. S. MacLean Gilmour in *The Interpreter's Bible* (New York: Abingdon-Cokesbury, 1952), Vol. VIII, p. 386: "It is possible that Jesus contemplated

the emergence of a situation in which His followers would have to resist aggression by use of force."

8. Cf. Rutenber, *The Dagger and the Cross* (New York: Fellowship Publications, 1950), p. 34.

Chapter 3

1. Article XVI, *Concordia Triglotta* (St. Louis: Concordia Publishing House, 1921), p. 51.
2. Article III, *ibid.*, p. 175.
3. Article XVI, *ibid.*, p. 331.
4. Cf. "How Far Secular Authority Extends," *Works of Martin Luther* (Philadelphia: A. J. Holman Company and the Castle Press, 1932), Vol. III, p. 270: "But when a prince is in the wrong, are his people bound to follow him then too? I answer, No, for it is no one's duty to do wrong; we ought to obey God Who desires the right, rather than men. How is it, when the subjects do not know whether the prince is in the right or not? I answer, As long as they cannot know, nor find out by any possible means, they may obey without peril to their souls. For in such a case one must apply the law of Moses, when he writes in Exodus xxi, that a murderer who has unknowingly and involuntarily killed a man shall be delivered by fleeing to a city of refuge and by the judgment of the congregation. For whichever side is defeated, whether it be in the right or in the wrong, must accept it as a punishment from God; but whichever side wars and wins, in such ignorance, must regard their battle as though one fell from the roof and killed another, and leave the matter to God. . . ."
5. "That Soldiers Too, Can Be Saved," *ibid.*, Vol. V, pp. 34–74.
6. *Ibid.*, Vol II, p. 50.
7. *Ibid.*, Vol. II, p. 51.
8. *Ibid.*, Vol. V, pp. 156–158.
9. Cf. H. Richard Klann, "Luther on War and Revolution," in *Concordia Theological Monthly*, May 1954, pp. 353–366.
10. Cf. L. J. Roehm, "The Christian's Attitude Towards His Government and on War," Reprint from *Concordia Theological Monthly*, May 1941, pp. 7–9.
11. *Loci Theologici*, edited by Preuss (Berlin: Sumtibus Gust. Schlawitz, 1866), Vol. VI, p. 507.
12. *Ibid.*, p. 509: *"Ne adversus eos, qui justis injuris lacessiti bellum nobis inferunt, ad arma properemus* (There should be a checkup to ascertain that the enemy has not been aroused through our own fault). . . ."
13. *Ibid.*, pp. 509–510.
14. Tract No. 20 (New York City: American Lutheran Publicity Bureau).
15. Louis J. Roehm, *op. cit.*, p. 23.
16. Cf. Otto E. Sohn, "Keep Them from Evil," *The Lutheran Witness*, May 1, 1951, p. 140.
17. Cf. "We Are at War," *The Cresset*, January 1942.
18. In *The Lutheran Chaplain*, 1946.

19. "The Power of Uplifted Hands," a sermon study (Chicago: The Army and Navy Commission).

20. "God's Call to Duty," a sermon study (Chicago: The Army and Navy Commission).

21. "A Service of Song and Prayer on the Day of Victory," for use in The Lutheran Church—Missouri Synod.

22. Paul F. Bente, "Suggested Sermon Material" (Department of Missionary Education and Publicity, The Lutheran Church—Missouri Synod).

23. Issued under the auspices of the Army and Navy Commission and printed by Concordia Publishing House, St. Louis.

24. Cf. *The Evangelical Christian*, September 1943.

25. "The Open Forum," *The American Lutheran*, September 1944.

26. An editorial, "The Russian Terror," *The Cresset*, June 1939.

27. *Ibid.*, January 1940.

28. *Ibid.*, June 1940.

29. Theodore Graebner in *The Lutheran Witness*, August 11, 1945.

30. *Ibid.*, December 30, 1947. Cf. "The Communist Menace," *ibid.*, August 27, 1946.

31. *St. Paul's College Courier*, Concordia, Missouri, June 1945.

32. *Noticiero Luterano*, May 1945: *"El Presidente Roosevelt era miembro de la Iglesia Anglicano or Episcopal, y siempre trato todos sus asuntos del punto de vista cristiano."*

33. In *The American Lutheran*, May 1945.

34. The sermon was based on the text from II Sam. 3:38, "Know ye not that there is a prince and a great man fallen this day in Israel?"

35. *E.g.*, the frontispiece of *The American Lutheran*, September 1944.

36. Abundant substantiation for these statements and those following can be found in the series of sermon books published by Concordia Publishing House, 1940–46.

37. Cf. "Keep America Christian!", *For Christ and Country*, p. 190: "Yet history testifies that there is one inner loss which is final that can remove national glory forever and permanently reduce any country, however rich and powerful. That deadliest danger is unbelief. . . . God's Truth . . . warns, 'The nation and kingdom that will not serve shall perish.'"

38. "Father, Forgive Them—and Us!", *Victory Through Christ*, p. 330. Cf. "Lord, Teach America to Pray!", *America, Turn to Christ*, p. 251: "[We should not] ask God to damn Hitler and Hirohito, the people of Germany and Japan, to the deepest hell; we are to plead for our enemies, asking the Almighty to lead them to Christ and for His sake to forgive them."

39. Cf. A. C. Mueller, "Children and War," *The Teacher's Quarterly*, January-March 1943.

40. "Hope for Peace Revives," *Lutheran Witness*, December 11, 1951, p. 409.

41. "The Balance of Power," *ibid.*, January 8, 1952, pp. 8–9.

42. "Korea," *ibid.*, July 25, 1950, p. 232.

43. Psa. 34:14; also cf. "Working for World Peace," *ibid.*, June 24, 1952, p. 9.

44. "The Brutalizing Effect of War," *Lutheran Witness*, October 3, 1950, p. 20.

45. "Is Survival Enough?", March 1951, pp. 1–2.

46. "Korea in Retrospect," *ibid.*, September 1951, pp. 2–3.
47. "The Christian Soldier," *ibid.*, October 1950, pp. 1–3.
48. The Church in Wartime," *ibid.*, September 1950, pp.4–5.
49. *Proceedings of the Forty-second Regular Convention of The Lutheran Church—Missouri Synod* (St. Louis: Concordia, 1953), p. 743.
50. In *Concordia Theological Monthly*, February 1955, pp. 127–128.
51. *The Lutheran*, November 19–December 17, 1941.
52. *Ibid.*, October 4, 1939.
53. Rev. Douglas Conrad, "Canada at War," *The Lutheran*, November 8, 1939.
54. *The Lutheran*, January 17, 1940.
55. The statement by the Executive Board was issued in January 1940, and comment was offered by Dr. Paul H. Krauss in *The Lutheran*.
56. Cf. *The Lutheran*, September 18, 25, 1940.
57. Ramme, in an open letter in *The Lutheran*, August 6, 1941, submitted that the word "right" in the Sixteenth Article of the Augsburg Confession should be interpreted as "privilege, not duty or responsibility."
58. "What Did Luther Think?", *The Lutheran*, October 9, 1940.
59. *Ibid.*, No. 36, p. 31.
60. Cf. *The Lutheran*, April 30, 1941.
61. Cf. *The Lutheran Church Quarterly*, April 1946.
62. The inclusion of references to the early Church Fathers in this section does not imply that they are to be regarded as exponents of Roman Catholicism. Their position on war would be more in accord with that of modern pacifist groups. Here our concern is with the historical development of the "just war" idea.
63. Cf. G. J. Heering, *The Fall of Christianity* (New York: Fellowship Publications, 1943), p. 25.
64. "For Caesar's soldiers possess nothing which they can lose more precious than their life, while our love goes out to that eternal love which God will give us by His might." In *Apology*, quoted by Heering, p. 25.
65. Part II, Canon 16, quoted by Bainton in *Social Action*, January 15, 1945.
66. Cf. *Contra Celsum*, quoted by Heering, p. 27.
67. Bainton, *op. cit.*, p. 14.
68. Cf. Heering, p. 34.
69. *Canons of Synod of Arles*, quoted by Heering, p. 35.
70. Athanasius: *Epistle to Ammonius*, quoted by De Jong, *Dienstweigerung*, p. 50, quoted by Heering, p. 36.
71. *De Officiis*, quoted by Heering, p. 36.
72. Cf. Thomas F. Doyle, "To War or Not to War," *The Catholic World*, December 1939: The "Ten Commandments" released by the German Ministry of Propaganda and Public Entertainment were said to express the attitude of the Roman Catholic Church: "1. Fight chivalrously, without unnecessary brutality. 2. A soldier must be uniformed. 3. A soldier must spare the life of any opponent who surrenders. 4. Treat prisoners humanely. 5. Refrain from the use of dumdum bullets. 6. Respect the Red Cross. 7. Spare the civil population unnecessary hardships and refrain from plundering. 8. Respect the neutrality of non-combatant states. 9. On capture, give name and identification, but nothing respecting army organization. 10. Report violations of these principles by the enemy."

73. Printed in *The Catholic World,* December 1939.
74. On August 24, 1939.
75. Cf. *America,* January 31 and March 7, 1942.
76. "The War, What Else But War?", *The Catholic World,* October 1939, p. 1.
77. "Churchmen and War," *ibid.,* February 1940, p. 4.
78. "We Fight in Their War? Why?", *America,* October 14, 1939, pp. 6–7.
79. "War May Be in Europe While America Is at Peace," *ibid.,* November 4, 1939, pp. 88–89.
80. "Steps That Lead to War," *ibid.,* January 6, 1940, pp. 340–341.
81. "All Will Be Lost by War," *ibid.,* June 29, 1940, p. 317.
82. Cf. articles that appeared in *America* in October 1941, in which the President's speech against the Axis powers on September 11 was called a declaration of war, and the fear was expressed that democracy was disappearing as the Chief Executive was exerting dictatorial powers.
83. *The Catholic World,* October 1945.
84. *Ibid.,* January 1946.
85. *America,* December 20, 1941.
86. *Ibid.,* August 4, 1945.
87. *Ibid.,* October 12, 1940.
88. *Theological Studies,* September 1944.
89. Reported in the issue of March 20, 1945.
90. *Catholic World,* September 1945.
91. *America,* July 7, 1945.
92. *The Commonweal,* March 22, 1946.
93. Cf. Robert Sencourt, "The War and the Church," *The Catholic World,* November 1939.
94. Cf. *The Catholic World,* March 1940.
95. Cf. *Newsweek,* September 9, 1940.
96. Cf. *The Catholic World,* October 1940.
97. Cf. Robert A. Graham, "What Kind of Peace Does the Pope Ask For?", *America,* June 24, pp. 315–316.
98. "The Hierarchy Speaks on the Issues of the Day," *ibid.,* Nov. 29, 1941, pp. 201.
99. Daniel J. Saunders in *Theological Studies,* March 1945, p. 35.
100. In *War Is My Parish* (Milwaukee: Bruce, 1944), p. 6.
101. *Ibid.,* p. 2.
102. *Ibid.,* p. 3.
103. Cf. Archbishop Francis J. Spellman, *The Road to Victory* (New York: Charles Scribner's Sons, 1942).
104. "Padre," *They Told It to a Chaplain* (New York: Vantage, 1953), pp. 91–92.
105. Cf. editorial, *ibid.,* July 4, 1953, p. 357.
106. Cf. Bainton, *op. cit.,* p. 24.
107. *Ibid.,* pp. 24–25.
108. Cf. Wallace Hancock, "The Non-Theological Foundations of Christian Pacifism," in *Fellowship,* June 1953.
109. Clifford F. Morehouse, "Let Us Give Thanks," *The Living Church,* August 19, 1945, p. 8.

110. Reported in The St. Louis *Globe-Democrat*, February 5, 1941.

111. Cf. "Churchman Militant," *Newsweek*, January 15, 1945.

112. H. Straton Hillyer, "Jesus, Exgesis, and War," *Anglican Review*, January 1944.

113. *Institutes*, Vol. IV, No. 20, p. 11.

114. Cf. Kerr, *A Compend of the Institutes of the Christian Religion* (Philadelphia: Presbyterian Board of Education, 1939), p. 208.

115. Cf. Heering, *op. cit.*, p. 60.

116. Cf. Bainton, *op. cit.*, p. 26.

117. In *England Under the Stuarts* (New York: Putnam, 1938), p. 219.

118. In *The Religious Digest*, March 1942. Taken from Robert Hastings Nichols, "War . . . Its Causes . . . and Cure . . . The Church in the War," *The Presbyterian Tribune*, Vol. 14, No. 78, pp. 1–7.

119. In *The Presbyterian Survey*, January 1942.

120. In *The Presbyterian*, January 25, 1940.

121. In this review of A. J. Muste's book, *Non-violence in an Aggressive World*, some scepticism was expressed concerning the thoroughness of the author's renunciation of Marxism-Leninism in his return to Christianity. Cf. *The Presbyterian*, May 16, 1940.

122. *Ibid.*, June 13, 1940.

123. Cf. "The Bible and the War," *ibid.*, July 18, 1940.

124. *Ibid.*, August 8, 1940.

125. Issue of February 4, 1950.

126. Cf. *Presbyterian Life*, February 3, 1951.

127. E.g., Gerald Winrod, editor of *The Defender*.

128. Cf. *Moody Monthly*, May and October 1943.

129. James M. Gray, "What the Bible Teaches About War and the Christian's Attitude in the Present Crisis," *ibid.*, Vol. XLVI, No. 1, pp. 5, 6.

130. The preaching of the Gospel is far more successful and God-pleasing than the destructive "liberations" of our armies, according to William Boyle. Cf. the editorial, *ibid.*, March 1953, p. 510.

131. Cf. editorial "But God," *ibid.*, April 1954, p. 21.

132. Cf. Neve, *History of Christian Thought* (Philadelphia: Muhlenberg Press, 1946), Vol. II, p. 20.

133. Cf. Engelder, *Popular Symbolics* (St. Louis: Concordia Publishing House, 1934), pp. 230ff.

134. "General Conference of 1944," *The Christian Advocate*, May 18, 1944, p. 5.

135. Pertinent reference was made to the Oxford Conference: "War is a particular demonstration of the power of sin in this world, and a defiance of the righteousness of God as revealed in Jesus Christ and Him crucified. No justification of war should be allowed to conceal or minimize this fact."

136. Georgia Harkness, "God and the War," *The Christian Advocate*, September 7, 1944, p. 6; and following issues.

137. Cf. Articles like John Foster Dulles, "The Churches and the Peace," *The Christian Advocate*, February 8, 1945, pp. 11, 12; and Roy L. Smith, "Toward Winning the Peace," *ibid.*, January 27, 1944, p. 3.

138. Today these are the very fears expressed by even the non-Communist nations in Europe and Asia that we claim to be "protecting."

139. "A Christian Peace," *ibid.*, June 25, 1942, p. 6.

140. Roy L. Smith, "Terrorism Always Defeats the Terrorist," *ibid.*, July 27, 1944, p. 3.

141. *Ibid.*, November 9, 1944.

142. "The Church and the Third World War," *ibid.*, November 30, 1944, pp. 9–10.

143. Roy L. Smith, "Preachers at Peace Conference," *ibid.*, February 8, 1945, pp. 3–4.

144. *Ibid.*, December 16, 1943.

145. "Bombed Babies," *ibid.*, March 2, 1944, p. 3.

146. *Ibid.*, February 17, 1944, p. 4.

147. *Ibid.*, January 29, 1942, p. 4.

148. "The Courage of True Americanism," *ibid.*, March 29, 1945, p. 3.

149. *Ibid.*, March 23, 1944.

150. *Ibid.*, September 21, 1944.

151. *Ibid.*, January 4, 1945. Compare, in contrast, the attitude of the International Round Tables of Christian leaders at Princeton in July 1943, as cited in *Time*, July 26, 1943. "They want no postwar military line-up of victorious big powers; they seek an all-nation world body instead."

152. Roy L. Smith, *The Christian Advocate*, January 11, 1945, p. 3.

153. "War Blame, War Horrors or Salvation?", *ibid.*, February 2, 1945, pp. 6–7.

154. "A Prayer for the Times," *ibid.*, January 20, 1944, p. 5.

155. T. A. Stafford, "A Prayer for Victory," *The Christian Advocate*, January 20, 1944, p. 12.

156. Andrew Cecil, "Is the U. S. Imperialistic?", *Motive*, March 1951.

157. Cf. The Dort Confession, Article XIII, quoted in Engelder, *op. cit.*, p. 262.

158. In *Menno Simmons' Life and Writings* (Scottdale, Pa.: Mennonite Publishing House, 1945), p. 11.

159. Quoted by Robert Friedman in "An Anabaptist Ordinance on Nonresistance," *The Mennonite Quarterly Review*, April 1951, p. 116.

160. *Ibid.*, p. 125.

161. Quoted by John C. Wenger in "The Theology of Pilgrim Marpeck," *ibid.*, 1938, pp. 355–356.

162. Quoted by Melvin Gingerich in "The Mennonite Church in World War II, A Review and Evaluation," *ibid.*, July 1951, p. 183.

163. *Ibid.*, pp. 184ff.

164. Rufus D. Bowman, *Seventy Times Seventy* (Elgin, Ill.: Brethren Publishing House, 1945), p. 11.

165. *Ibid.*, pp. 13–14.

166. *Ibid.*, p. 34.

167. Cf. *Huntingdon Conference Minutes*, 1944, p. 52, quoted by Bowman, *op. cit.*, pp. 34–35.

168. Bowman, *op. cit.*, p. 49.

169. Cf. Bainton, *op. cit.*, p. 27.

170. Guy F. Hershberger, "Biblical Nonresistance and Modern Pacifism," *The Mennonite Quarterly Review*, July 1943, pp. 120–121.
171. In *Friends and War*, quoted by G. J. Heering, *op. cit.*, p. 68.
172. Cf. his *Solemn Review of the Custom of War* (1814), as quoted in Hershberger, *op. cit.*, p. 121.
173. Cf. W. W. Van Kirk, *Religion Renounces War* (Chicago: 1934), p. 12, as quoted in Hershberger, *op. cit.*, p. 124.
174. Van Kirk, *op. cit.*, p. 10, as quoted in Hershberger, *op. cit.*, p. 124.
175. Van Kirk, *op. cit.*, pp. 118–119, as quoted in Hershberger, *op. cit.*, p. 125.
176. Quoted by Don E. Smucker in "The Theological Basis for Christian Pacifism," *Mennonite Quarterly Review*, July 1953, p. 164.
177. "Atrocity Stories—1944," *Fellowship*, March 1944.
178. Published on February 4, 1944.
179. As stated in The New York *Herald-Tribune*, January 29, 1944.
180. Cf. the Asiatic Exclusion Laws.
181. In *Fellowship*, March 1944.
182. In *The Sunday Express* of London, November 28, 1943.
183. In *Fellowship*, March 1944.
184. *Ibid.*, November 1944.
185. *Ibid.*, February 1945.
186. Released on May 8, 1945.
187. In *Fellowship*, March 1946.
188. "Korean Urges Food, Not Bombs," *Fellowship*, March 1951, p. 21.

Chapter 4

1. Arthur F. Steinke, *The Bible and War* (Brooklyn: The Studio Press, 1941), p. 31.
2. Cf. Charles A. Beard, *President Roosevelt and the Coming of the War, 1941*, (New Haven: Yale University Press, 1948).
3. Even those who have written in defense of our wartime President have admitted as much. Cf. Basil Rauch, *Roosevelt from Munich to Pearl Harbor* (New York: Creative Age Press, 1950).
4. Quoted by William Henry Chamberlin in "The Bankruptcy of a Policy," in Harry Elmer Barnes, editor, *Perpetual War for Perpetual Peace* (Caldwell, Idaho: Caxton Printers, 1953), pp. 489–490.
5. Harry E. Yarnell (retired) on July 7, and Admiral Standley (subsequently our Ambassador to the Soviet Union) on October 12.
6. For a thorough and unprejudiced account of such tactics, cf. "The Battle against Intervention," in Wayne S. Cole, *America First* (Madison: University of Wisconsin Press, 1953).
7. Cf. the widely publicized book *Under Cover*, by John Roy Carlson (whose real name was Avedis Derounian, and who was a private sleuth for Friends of Democracy, Inc.), (Cleveland and New York: World, 1943).
8. Cf. "Is Lindbergh a Nazi?", a pamphlet written and distributed by Leon M. Birkhead, National Director of Friends of Democracy, Inc. Lindbergh was

called a "hero only to the disciples of Adolph Hitler" and it was said that "he
has become the American voice of the Berlin Propaganda Ministry." Because
a newspaper in Hamburg had hailed him as a "real" American, he was
described as an apologist for Nazism. Excerpts from Hitler's speeches were
torn out of context and put alongside those of Lindbergh in an attempt to
prove that the latter followed the Nazi line.

9. Cf. *The Grand Alliance* (Boston: Houghton, 1950), p. 23: "The President
is determined that we shall win the war together. Make no mistake about
that."

10. Cf. William Henry Chamberlin, *America's Second Crusade* (Chicago: Regnery, 1950), p. 130.

11. *Ibid.,* p. 168.

12. The principal spokesmen for this "revisionist" school have been Charles
Beard and Charles Tansill. George Morgenstern defended their thesis as early
as 1947, however. Cf. his *Pearl Harbor* (New York: Devin-Adair, 1947).

13. It would be more pertinent to expose the aims of our erstwhile ally, Communist Russia. Cf. William Henry Chamberlin, *Blueprint for World Conquest*
(Chicago: Regnery, 1946), and David J. Dallin, *Soviet Russia's Foreign Policy,
1939–1942* (New Haven: Yale University Press, 1942).

14. Cf. Chamberlin, *ibid.,* p. 136.

15. Why we envisioned no obstacles in postwar trade relations with another
totalitarian power—namely, Soviet Russia—is not at all clear.

16. Cf. Bernard Iddings Bell, *A Man Can Live* (New York: Harper and
Brothers, 1947), p. 11: "Well, we defeated our enemies but in doing it we
well-night obliterated European civilization, as well as that of most of Asia;
we destroyed the sovereignty of helpless little nations and gave them over to
be swallowed up by those titanic neighbors who had sworn to protect their
integrity."

17. Consider the Communist infiltration into the Canadian government. Cf.
*Report of Royal Commission to Investigate Disclosures of Secret Information,
to Unauthorized Persons* (Ottawa: King's Printer).

18. *Loci Theologici,* edited by Preuss (Berlin: Sumtibus Gust. Schlawitz,
1863), Vol. VI, pp. 512–13.

19. Cf. F. J. P. Veale, *Advance to Barbarism* (Appleton, Wis.: Nelson, 1953),
pp. 131–138.

20. Veale, *op. cit.,* p. 122.

21. Cf. his book *Bombing Vindicated* (London: Bles, 1944), pp. 47, 74.

22. Cf. his book *Bomber Offensive* (London: Collins, 1947), quoted by Veale,
op. cit., p. 126.

23. Cf. The Rt. Hon. Lord Hankey, *Politics, Trials and Errors* (Chicago:
Regnery, 1950), pp. 125–126: "It embittered the war, rendered inevitable a
fight to the finish, banged the door to any possibility of either side offering
terms or opening up negotiations, gave the Germans and the Japanese the
courage of despair, strengthened Hitler's position as Germany's 'only hope,'
aided by Goebbels' propaganda, and made inevitable the Normandy landing
and the subsequent terribly exhausting and destructive advance through North
France, Belgium, Luxembourg, Holland and Germany. The lengthening of the
war enabled Stalin to occupy the whole of eastern Europe, to ring down the

iron curtain and so to realize at one sweep a large instalment of his avowed aims against so-called capitalism, in which he includes social democracy. By disposing of all the more competent administrators in Germany and Japan this policy rendered treaty-making impossible after the war and retarded recovery and reconstruction, not only in Germany and Japan, but everywhere else. It may also prove to have poisoned our future relations with ex-enemy countries. Not only the enemy countries, but nearly all countries were bled white by this policy, which has left us all, except the United States of America, impoverished and in dire straits. Unfortunately also, these policies, so contrary to the spirit of the Sermon on the Mount, did nothing to strengthen the moral position of the Allies."

24. Cf. review of *Hiroshima Diary in Newsweek*, August 8, 1955.

25. Thus, Robert Hutchins, at that time Chancellor of the University of Chicago, said that by our decision to drop the atom bomb we forfeited any claim that we might still have to moral leadership in the world.

26. Cf. *Lutheran Standard*, August 27, 1955, p. 2.

27. In the opinion of former Ambassador William C. Bullitt, "no more unnecessary, disgraceful, and potentially disastrous document has ever been signed by a President of the United States." Cf. *Life* Magazine, October 13, 1947. William Henry Chamberlin could not find "one positive, worthwhile contribution to European revival and stability in the sordid deals of Yalta, only imperialist power politics at its worst." *Op. cit.*, p. 216.

28. Cf. Freda Utley, *The China Story* (Chicago: Regnery, 1951).

29. In condemning the Morgenthau Plan, Marshall Knappen called it a "concession to those elements in the American public motivated by a desire for revenge on their enemies." He denounced the whole scheme as stupid and wasteful: "Aside from the matter of the broken promises, it would cost thousands of American lives and millions of dollars in increased occupation costs . . . it was worse than a crime. It was a blunder . . . it destroyed the effect of months of hard work on the part of our psychological warfare units, as it seemed to prove Goebbels all too correct in his contention that the loss of the war meant slavery for Germany. Weary men returning from the field reported that the Germans fought with twice their previous determination after the announcement of the Morgenthau policy." *And Call It Peace* (Chicago: University of Chicago Press, 1947), p. 54.

30. Cf. Otto Von Kranzbuehler, "Nuremberg as a Legal Problem," in *German Views of the War Trials* (Dallas: Southern Methodist University Press, 1955), pp. 115–116.

31. Veale, *op. cit.*, p. 169.

32. Montgomery Belgion, *Victors' Justice* (Chicago: Regnery, 1949), *passim.*

33. Cf. Veale, *op. cit.*, pp. 217–241.

34. According to estimates prepared by the information section of NATO, these prisoners included 2,000,000 Germans, 370,000 Japanese, 180,000 Roumanians, 200,000 Hungarians, and 63,520 Italians. Forty per cent of these were regarded as dead by 1952. Cf. Veale, *op. cit.*, p. 238.

35. *Victors' Justice*, p. 80.

36. Cf. R. Thompson, *Cry Korea* (Macdonald), pp. 258–259, quoted by Capt. Russell Grenfell in *Unconditional Hatred* (New York: Devin-Adair, 1954), p. 189.

37. *Op. cit.*, p. 273.

38. If we are searching for principles that should determine our attitude toward the state, also, in wartime, we will do well to keep in mind these excerpts from the address which Bishop Berggrav of Norway delivered before the Lutheran World Federation Assembly in 1952:

1. It is a positively frightful misrepresentation of Lutheran doctrine to assert that "wild conquerors" or "despotic revolutionists" should "come into the possession of power." It is high time that such views be plainly labeled as heretical.

2. Luther knew that instances might occur where Christians would have to refuse to obey the orders of their government. . . . When a government becomes lawless and acts with arbitrary despotism, the result is a demonic condition, that is to say, the government is godless. To obey such a satanic government would be nothing short of sinful. Here the text Acts 5:29 . . . applies: "We ought to obey God rather than men."

3. Luther rejected the idea that the Church as such should ever use forcible means against the government. The Church's purpose, he said, is to preach the Gospel and, in case of necessity, to suffer martyrdom. This means, on the one hand, that the Church must not organize or conduct revolutions, not even against a tyrant. But on the other hand, it also means positively that the Church has the sacred duty, come what may, fearlessly to proclaim to the unjust ruler the unvarnished truth set forth in the Gospel and the Law. The Church is no institute of edification where one is safe from all danger. In this world of despotism and injustice, the Lutheran Church will always be something dangerous or else it will cease to be a Christian church.

4. The Church must demand the undiminished freedom to proclaim the Word of God and to exercise Christian love in the service of men. . . . The Church must not allow itself to be exploited by the state for political purposes. The Church must not become a tool of power politics. . . . The state must force nothing upon anyone, whether child or adult, that is contrary to God's clear commandments. A state which arrogates to itself the right to determine what is good and what is evil, must logically think of itself as an institute of salvation; and this is equivalent to the deification of the state. . . .

Quoted from "State and Church Today," *The Proceedings of the Second Assembly of The Lutheran World Federation*, pp. 76–85.

Chapter 5

1. Cf. I Kings 20:31.
2. Veale, *op. cit.*, p. 134.
3. *Ibid.*, p. 42.
4. *Ibid.*, p. 91.
5. Cf. his celebrated essay "Modern Man Is Obsolete."

6. Cf. Edwin McNeill Poteat, *Last Reprieve?* (New York: Harper & Bros., 1946), p. 25.

7. *Ibid.*, pp. 19–20.

8. *America and the Atomic Age* (Chicago: University of Chicago, 1951), p. 16.

9. Cf. "Morals of Making the H-bomb," *Newsweek*, August 2, 1954, p. 25.

10. Gordon Dean, *Report on the Atom* (New York: Alfred Knopf, 1953), pp. 123–124.

11. In *Bulletin of the Atomic Scientists*, June 1954, as quoted by Elmer Davis, in his book *Two Minutes Till Midnight* (Indianapolis: Bobbs-Merrill, 1955), pp. 23–24.

12. Cf. *United States News and World Report*, August 12, 1955, pp. 58–65.

13. Cf. *Washington Newsletter* of the Friends Committee on National Legislation, Washington, D. C., October 1955.

14. Quoted by Edward Leroy Long, Jr., in *The Christian Response to the Atomic Crisis* (Philadelphia: Westminster, 1950), p. 96.

15. In *Atomic Weapons and Armies* (New York: Praeger, 1955), pp. 214–215.

16. Cf. "War Unlikely During Soviet-Free World Balance," in *Washington University Alumni Bulletin*, October, 1955, pp. 4, 17.

17. Cf. *The Christian Century*, December 5, 1954, p. 1509.

18. Cf. The Chicago *Sun-Times*, January 4, 1955, p. 12.

19. In "Nuclear Weapons and Genetics," *Fellowship*, September 1955.

20. Cf. "Across the Atlantic in 30 Minutes," *U. S. News and World Report*, January 20, 1956.

21. Cf. *Newsweek*, September 12, 1955, p. 70.

22. In the issue of April 21, 1954, p. 485.

23. Smucker, "The Theological Basis for Christian Pacifism," *op. cit.*, p. 180.

24. Long, *op. cit.*, p. 14.

25. According to their observations, the smoke cloud from an H-bomb explosion took the form of a cross as it rose into the upper atmosphere. Cf. *Newsweek*, April 26, 1954, p. 89.

26. Cf. *Peace Action Letter*, The Chicago Peace Committee, 166 West Washington St., Chicago, Ill., April 1956.

27. Available from The American Council on Education, 1785 Massachusetts Avenue, N.W., Washington 6, D.C.

28. Modern Library Edition (New York: Random House), p. 502.

29. Cf. the editorial "Russia Deserts Theory of Inevitable War," *Christian Century*, November 9, 1955, p. 1292.

Bibliography

Barnes, Harry Elmer, ed., *Perpetual War for Perpetual Peace*. Caldwell, Idaho: Caxton Printers, 1953.

Beard, Charles A., *President Roosevelt and the Coming of the War, 1941*. New Haven: Yale University Press, 1948.

Belgion, Montgomery, *Victors' Justice*. Chicago: Regnery, 1949.

Benedict, Marion J., *The God of the Old Testament in Relation to War*. New York: Teachers College, Columbia University, 1927.

Boettner, Lorraine, *The Christian Attitude Toward War*. Grand Rapids: Eerdmans Publishing Co., 1940.

Bowman, Rufus D., *Seventy Times Seven*. Elgin, Ill., Brethren Publishing House, 1945.

Brunner, Emil, *Christianity and Civilization*. New York: Charles Scribner's Sons, 1949.

Bullitt, William C., *The Great Globe Itself*. New York: Charles Scribner's Sons, 1946.

Cadoux, C. J., *Early Christian Attitude Toward War*. London: G. Allen, 1940.

Chamberlin, William H., *America's Second Crusade*. Chicago: Regnery, 1950.

—— Beyond Containment. Chicago: Regnery, 1953.

Churchill, Winston. *The Grand Alliance*. Boston: Houghton-Mifflin, 1950.

Cole, Wayne S., *America First, the Battle Against Intervention, 1940–41*. Madison: University of Wisconsin Press, 1953.

Davis, Elmer, *Two Minutes Till Midnight*. Indianapolis: Bobbs-Merrill, 1955.

Dean, Gordon, *Report on the Atom*. New York: Alfred Knopf, 1953.

Engelder, Theodore, *Popular Symbolics*. St. Louis: Concordia, 1934.

Gerhard, John, *Loci Theologici, Preuss.* Berlin: Sumtibus. Gust. Schlawitz, 1866.

Grenfell, Captain Russell, *Unconditional Hatred.* New York: Devin-Adair, 1954.

Heering, G. J., *The Fall of Christianity.* New York: Fellowship Publications, 1943.

Johnson, Walter, *The Battle Against Isolation.* Chicago: University of Chicago Press, 1944.

Jones, Rufus, editor, *The Church, the Gospel and War.* New York: Harper and Brothers, 1948.

Knappen, Marshall, *And Call It Peace.* Chicago: University of Chicago Press, 1947.

Knudson, A. C., *The Philosophy of War and Peace.* New York: Abingdon-Cokesbury, 1947.

Kranzbuehler, Otto von, *German Views of the War Trials.* Dallas: Southern Methodist University Press, 1955.

Lindsay, A. D., *The Moral Teachings of Jesus.* New York: Harper and Brothers, 1937.

Long, Edward Leroy, Jr., *The Christian Response to the Atomic Bomb.* Philadelphia: Westminster Press, 1950.

Miksche, Lieutenant-Colonel F. O., *Atomic Weapons and Armies.* New York: Praeger, 1955.

Morgenstern, George, *Pearl Harbor.* New York: Devin-Adair, 1947.

Neve, J. L., *History of Christian Thought.* Philadelphia: Muhlenberg Press, 1946.

Niebuhr, Reinhold, *Christianity and Power Politics.* New York: Charles Scribner's Sons, 1950.

Poteat, Edwin McNeill, *Last Reprieve?* New York: Harper and Brothers, 1946.

Ramsay, Paul, *Basic Christian Ethics.* New York: Charles Scribner's Sons, 1950.

Rauch, Basil, *Roosevelt From Munich to Pearl Harbor.* New York: Creative Age Press, 1950.

Reu-Buehring, M., *Christian Ethics.* Columbus: The Lutheran Book Concern, 1935.

Roehm, L. J., *The Christian's Attitude Toward His Government and on War*, reprint from *Concordia Theological Monthly*, May 1941. St. Louis: Concordia Publishing House, 1941.

Rutenber, Culbert G., *The Dagger and the Cross*. New York: Fellowship Publications, 1950.

Spaight, J. M., *Bombing Vindicated*. London: Bles, 1944.

Steinke, Arthur F., *The Bible and War*. Brooklyn: The Studio Press, 1941.

Tansill, Charles Callan, *Back Door to War, the Roosevelt Foreign Policy, 1933–41*. Chicago: Regnery, 1952.

Utley, Freda, *The China Story*. Chicago: Regnery, 1951.

—— *The High Cost of Vengeance*. Chicago: Regnery, 1949.

Veale, F. J. P., *Advance to Barbarism*. Appleton, Wisconsin: Nelson, 1953.